Managing Products and Services

PS14

CARING FOR THE CUSTOMER

Published for
The National Examining Board for Supervision and Management

by
Pergamon Open Learning

Pergamon Open Learning
An imprint of Butterworth-Heinemann Ltd
Linacre House, Jordan Hill, Oxford OX2 8DP

ℛ A member of the Reed Elsevier plc group

OXFORD   LONDON   BOSTON
MUNICH   NEW DELHI   SINGAPORE   SYDNEY
TOKYO   TORONTO   WELLINGTON

Reprinted 1995

A catalogue record for this book is available from the British Library

ISBN book only: 0 08 041818 X

Design and Production: Pergamon Open Learning

NEBSM Project Manager: Pam Sear
Author: Howard Senter
Editor: Ian Bloor
Series Editor: Diana Thomas

Typeset by BPC Techset Ltd, Exeter
Printed in Great Britain by BPC Wheatons Ltd, Exeter

CONTENTS

USER GUIDE

1 Welcome to the User Guide

Hello and welcome to the NEBSM Super Series second edition (Super Series 2) flexible training programme.

It is quite likely that you are a supervisor, a team leader, an assistant manager, a foreman, a section head, a first-line or a junior manager and have people working under you. The Super Series programme is ideal for all, whatever the job title, who are on or near that first rung of the management ladder. By choosing this programme we believe that you have made exactly the right decision when it comes to meeting your own needs and those of your organization.

The purpose of this guide is to help you gain the maximum benefit both from this particular workbook and audio cassette and also from a full supervisory management training programme.

You should read the whole of this User Guide thoroughly before you start any work on the unit and use the information and advice to help plan your studies.

If you are new to the idea of studying or training by yourself or have never before worked with a tutor or trainer on an individual basis, you should pay particular attention to the section below about Open Learning and tutorial support.

If you are a trainer or tutor evaluating this material for use with prospective students or clients, we think you will also find the information given here useful as it will help you to prepare and conduct individual pre-course counselling and group briefing sessions.

2 Your Open Learning Programme

What do we mean by 'Open Learning'?

Let's start by looking at what is meant by 'Open Learning' and how it could affect the way you approach your studies.

Open Learning is a term used to describe a method of training where you, the learner, make most of the decisions about *how*, *when* and *where* you do your learning. To make this possible you need to have available material, written or prepared in a special way (such as this book and audio cassette) and then have access to Open Learning centres that have been set up and prepared to offer guidance and support as and when required.

Undertaking your self-development training by Open Learning allows you to fit in with priorities at work and at home and to build the right level of confidence and independence needed for success, even though at first it may take you a little while to establish a proper routine.

The workbook and audio cassette

Though this guide is mainly aimed at you as a first time user, it is possible that you are already familiar with the earlier editions of the Super Series. If that is the case, you should know that there are quite a few differences in the workbook and audio cassette, some of which were very successfully trialled in the last 12 units of the first edition. Apart from the more noticeable features such as changes in page layouts and more extensive use of colour and graphics, you will find activities, questions and assignments that are more closely related to work and more thought-provoking.

The amount of material on the cassette is, on average, twice the length of older editions and is considerably more integrated with the workbook. In fact, there are so many extras now that are included as standard that the average study time per unit has been increased by almost a third. You will find a useful summary of all workbook and cassette features in the charts below and on page vii.

Whether you are a first time user or not, the first step towards being a successful Open Learner is to be familiar and comfortable with the learning material. It is well worth spending a little of your initial study time scanning the workbook to see how it is structured, what the various sections and features are called and what they are designed to do.

This will save you a lot of time and frustration when you start studying as you will then be able to concentrate on the actual subject matter itself without the need to refer back to what you are supposed to be doing with each part.

At the outset you are assumed to have no prior knowledge or experience of the subject and can expect to be taken logically, step by step from start to finish of the learning programme. To help you take on new ideas and information, and to help you remember and apply them, you will come across many different and challenging self check tasks, activities, quizzes and questions which you should approach seriously and enthusiastically. These features are designed not only to make your learning easier and more interesting but to help you to apply what you are studying to your own work situation in a practical and down-to-earth way.

To help to scan the workbook and cassette properly, and to understand what you find, here is a summary of the main features:

The workbook

If you want:	Refer to:
To see which other Super Series 2 units can also help you with this topic	The Study links
An overview of every part of the workbook and how the book and audio cassette link together	The Unit map
A list of the main knowledge and skill outcomes you will gain from the unit	The Unit objectives
To check on your understanding of the subject and your progress as you work thorough each section	The Activities and Self checks
To test how much you have understood and learned of the whole unit when your studies are complete	The Quick quiz and Action checks
An assessment by a third party for work done and time spent on this unit for purposes of recognition, award or certification	The Unit assessment The Work-based assignment
To put some of the things learned from the unit into practice in your own work situation	The Action plan (where present)

If you want:	Refer to:
To start your study of the unit	The Introduction: Side one
To check your knowledge of the complete unit	The Quick quiz: Side one
To check your ability to apply what you have learned to 'real life' by listening to some situations and deciding what you should do or say	The Action checks: Side two

Managing your learning programme

When you feel you know your way around the material, and in particular appreciate the progress checking and assessment features, the next stage is to put together your own personal study plan and decide how best to study.

These two things are just as important as checking out the material; they are also useful time savers and give you the satisfaction of feeling organized and knowing exactly where you are going and what you are trying to achieve.

You have already chosen your subject (this unit) so you should now decide when you need to finish the unit and how much time you must spend to make sure you reach your target.

To help you to answer these questions, you should know that each workbook and audio cassette will probably take about *eight* to *ten* hours to complete; the variation in time allows for different reading, writing and study speeds and the length and complexity of any one subject.

Don't be concerned if it takes you longer than these average times, especially on your first unit, and always keep in mind that the objective of your training is understanding and applying the learning, not competing in a race.

Experience has shown that each unit is best completed over a two-week period with about *three* to *four* study hours spent on it in each week, and about *one* to *two* hours at each sitting. These times are about right for tackling a new subject and still keeping work and other commitments sensibly in balance.

Using these time guides you should set, and try to keep to, specific times, days, and dates for your study. You should write down what you have decided and keep it visible as a reminder. If you are studying more than one unit, probably as part of a larger training programme, then the compilation of a full, dated plan or schedule becomes even more important and might have to tie in with dates and times set by others, such as a tutor.

The next step is to decide where to study. If you are doing this training in conjunction with your company or organization this might be decided for you as most have quiet areas, training rooms, learning centres, etc., which you will be encouraged to use. If you are working at home, set aside a quiet corner where books and papers can be left and kept together with a comfortable chair and a simple writing surface. You will also need a note pad and access to cassette playing equipment.

When you are finally ready to start studying, presuming that you are feeling confident and organized after your preparations, you should follow the instructions given in the Unit Map and the Unit Objectives pages. These tell you to play the first part of Side one of the audio cassette, a couple of times is a good idea, then follow the cues back to the workbook.

You should then work through each workbook section doing all that is asked of you until you reach the final assessments. Don't forget to keep your eye on the Unit Map as you progress and try to finish each session at a sensible point in the unit, ideally at the end of a complete section or part. You should always start your next session by looking back, for at least ten to fifteen minutes, at the work you did in the previous session.

You are encouraged to retain any reports, work-based assignments or other material produced in conjunction with your work through this unit in case you wish to present these later as evidence for a competency award or accreditation of prior learning.

Help, guidance and tutorial support

The workbook and audio cassette have been designed to be as self-contained as possible, acting as your guide and tutor throughout your studies. However, there are bound to be times when you might not quite understand what the author is saying, or perhaps you don't agree with a certain point. Whatever the reason, we all need help and support from time to time and Open Learner's are no exception.

Help during Open Learning study can come in many forms, providing you are prepared to seek it out and use it:

● first of all you could help yourself. Perhaps you are giving up too easily. Go back over it and try again;

● or you could ask your family or friends. Even if they don't understand the subject, the act of discussing it sometimes clarifies things in your own mind;

● then there is your company trainer or superior. If you are training as part of a company scheme, and during work time, then help and support will probably have been arranged for you already. Help and advice under these circumstances are important, especially as they can help you interpret your studies through actual and relevant company examples;

● if you are pursuing this training on your own, you could enlist expert help from a local Open Learning centre or agency. Such organizations exist in considerable numbers throughout the UK, often linked to colleges and other training establishments. The National Examining Board for Supervision and Management (NEBSM or NEBS Management), has several hundred such centres and can provide not only help and support but full assessment and accreditation facilities if you want to pursue a qualification as part of your chosen programme.

The NEBSM Super Series second edition is a selection of workbook and audio cassette packages covering a wide range of supervisory and first line management topics.

Although the individual books and cassettes are completely self-contained and cover single subject areas, each belongs to one of the four modular groups shown. These groups can help you build up your personal development programme as you can easily see which subjects are related. The groups are also important if you undertake any NEBSM national award programme.

Managing Human Resources		
HR1	Supervising at Work	HR10 Managing Time
HR2	Supervising with Authority	HR11 Hiring People
HR3	Team Leading	HR12 Interviewing
HR4	Delegation	HR13 Training Plans
HR5	Workteams	HR14 Training Sessions
HR6	Motivating People	HR15 Industrial Relations
HR7	Leading Change	HR16 Employment and the Law
HR8	Personnel in Action	HR17 Equality at Work
HR9	Performance Appraisal	HR18 Work-based Assessment

Managing Information		
IN1	Communicating	IN7 Using Statistics
IN2	Speaking Skills	IN8 Presenting Figures
IN3	Orders and Instructions	IN9 Introduction to
IN4	Meetings		Information Technology
IN5	Writing Skills	IN10 Computers and
IN6	Project Preparation		Communication Systems

Managing Financial Resources		
FR1	Accounting for Money	FR4 Pay Systems
FR2	Control via Budgets	FR5 Security
FR3	Controlling Costs	

Managing Products and Services		
PS1	Controlling Work	PS8 Productivity
PS2	Health and Safety	PS9 Stock Control Systems
PS3	Accident Prevention	PS10 Stores Control
PS4	Ensuring Quality	PS11 Efficiency in the Office
PS5	Quality Techniques	PS12 Marketing
PS6	Taking Decisions	PS13 Caring for the Environment
PS7	Solving Problems	PS14 Caring for the Customer

While the contents have been thoroughly updated, many Super Series 2 titles remain the same as, or very similar to the first edition units. Where, through merger, rewrite or deletion title changes have also been made, this summary should help you. If you are in any doubt please contact Pergamon Open Learning direct.

First Edition	Second Edition

First Edition

Merged titles
105 Organization Systems and 106 Supervising in the System
100 Needs and Rewards and 101 Enriching Work
502 Discipline and the Law and 508 Supervising and the Law
204 Easy Statistics and 213 Descriptive Statistics
200 Looking at Figures and 202 Using Graphs
210 Computers and 303 Communication Systems

402 Cost Reduction and 405 Cost Centres
203 Method Study and 208 Value Analysis

Major title changes
209 Quality Circles
205 Quality Control

Deleted titles
406 National Economy/410 Single European Market

Second Edition

HR1 Supervising at Work
HR6 Motivating People
HR16 Employment and the Law
IN7 Using Statistics
IN8 Presenting Figures
IN10 Computers and Communication Systems
FR3 Controlling Costs
PS8 Productivity

PS4 Ensuring Quality
PS5 Quality Techniques

&NEBS Management

The NEBSM Super Series 2 Open Learning material is published by Pergamon Open Learning in conjunction with NEBS Management.

NEBS Management is the largest provider of management education, training courses and qualifications in the United Kingdom, operating through over 700 Centres. Many of these Centres offer Open Learning and can provide help to individual students.

Many thousands of students follow the Open Learning route with great success and gain NEBSM or other qualifications.

NEBSM maintains a twin track approach to Supervisory Management training offering knowledge-based awards at three levels:

● the NEBSM Introductory Award in Supervisory Management;
● the NEBSM Certificate in Supervisory Management;
● the NEBSM Diploma in Supervisory Management;

and competence based awards at two levels:

● the NEBSM NVQ in Supervisory Management at Level 3;
● the NEBSM NVQ in Management at Level 4.

Knowledge-based awards and Super Series 2

The *Introductory Award* requires a minimum of 30 hours of study and provides a grounding in the theory and practice of supervisory management. An agreed programme of up to five NEBSM Super Series 2 units plus a one-day workshop satisfactorily completed can lead to this Award. Pre-approved topic combinations exist for general, industrial and commercial options. Completed Super Series 2 units can be allowed as an exemption towards the full NEBSM Certificate.

The *Certificate in Supervisory Management* requires study of up to 23 NEBSM Super Series 2 units and participation in group activity or workshops. The assessment system includes work-based assignments, a case study, a project and an oral interview. The certificate is divided into four modules and each one may be completed separately.
A *Module Award* can be made on successful completion of each module, and when the assessments are satisfactorily completed the Certificate is awarded. Students will need to register with a NEBSM Centre in order to enter for an award; NEBSM can advise you.

The *Diploma in Supervisory Management* consists of the formulation and implementation of a Personal Development Plan plus a generic management core. The programme is assessed by means of a log book, case study/in tray exercises, project or presentation.

The NEBSM Super Series 2 Open Learning material is designed for use at Certificate level but can also be used for the Introductory Award and provide valuable background knowledge for the Diploma.

Competence-based programmes and Super Series 2

The **NEBSM NVQ in Supervisory Management Level 3** is based upon the seven units of competence produced by the Management Charter Initiative (MCI) in their publication *Supervisory Management Standards* of June 1992. It is recognized by the National Council for Vocational Qualifications (NCVQ) at Level 3 in their framework.

The **NEBSM NVQ in Management Level 4** is based upon the nine units of competence produced by MCI in their publication *Occupational Standards for Managers, Management 1 and Assessment Criteria* of April 1991. It is recognized by the National Council for Vocational Qualifications (NCVQ) at Level 4 in their framework.

Super Series 2 units can be used to provide the necessary underpinning knowledge, skills and understanding that are required to prepare yourself for competence-based assessment.

Working through Super Series 2 units cannot, by itself, provide you with everything you need to enter or be entered for competence assessment. This must come from a combination of skill, experience and knowledge gained both on and off the job.

You will also find many of the 47 Super Series 2 units of use in learning programmes for other National Vocational Qualifications (NVQs) which include elements of supervisory management. Please check with the relevant NVQ lead body for information on Units of Competence and underlying knowledge, skills and understanding.

Competence Match Chart

The Competence Match Chart overleaf illustrates which Super Series 2 titles provide background vital to the current MCI M1S Supervisory Management Standards. You will also find that there is similar matching at MCI M1, Management 1 Standards. This is shown on the chart on page xiii.

For more information about MCI contact:

Management Charter Initiative
Russell Square House
10–12 Russell Square
London
WC1B 5BZ

Progression

Many successful NEBSM students use their qualifications as stepping stones to other awards, both educational and professional. Recognition is given by a number of bodies for this purpose. Further details about this and other NEBSM matters can be obtained from:

NEBSM Information Officer
The National Examining Board for Supervision and Management
1 Giltspur Street
London
EC1A 9DD

Competence Match Chart MCI M1S

The chart shows matches of Super Series 2 titles with MCI M1S (Supervisory Management) Units of Competence. Titles indicated ● are directly relevant to MCI Units, those marked ◑ provide specific supporting information, and those listed ○ provide useful general background.

NEBSM Super Series 2 Titles		1	2	3	4	5	6	7
PS1	Controlling Output	◑	◑					
PS2	Health and Safety	●	○			○		
PS3	Accident Prevention	●	○			○		
PS4	Ensuring Quality	●	○					
PS5	Quality Techniques	●						
PS6	Taking Decisions	○	○			◑	◑	
PS7	Solving Problems	○	○			◑	●	
PS8	Productivity		◑			●		
PS9	Stock Control Systems		◑					
PS10	Stores Control		◑					
PS11	Efficiency in the Office		◑			◑		
PS12	Marketing	○						
PS13	Caring for the Environment	◑	◑			○	○	○
PS14	Caring for the Customer	◑	○			○		
HR1	Supervising at Work					●	●	
HR2	Supervising with Authority					●	●	
HR3	Team Leading					●	●	
HR4	Delegation				●	●	◑	
HR5	Workteams					●	●	
HR6	Motivating People					●	●	
HR7	Leading Change		◑			●		
HR8	Personnel in Action			●				
HR9	Performance Appraisal				●		●	
HR10	Managing Time		○		○			
HR11	Hiring People			●				
HR12	Interviewing			●	●	◑	●	
HR13	Training Plans				●			
HR14	Training Sessions				●			
HR15	Industrial Relations						●	
HR16	Employment and the Law			○			●	
HR17	Equality at Work			◑			●	
HR18	Work-based Assessment			○	●	●	○	○
FR1	Accounting for Money		●					
FR2	Control via Budgets		●					
FR3	Controlling Costs		●					
FR4	Pay Systems							
FR5	Security	◑	◑					
IN1	Communicating	○	○	○	○	○	○	●
IN2	Speaking Skills	○	○	○	○	○	○	●
IN3	Orders and Instructions	◑				●	●	
IN4	Meetings				○	●	◑	●
IN5	Writing Skills	○	◑			○	◑	○
IN6	Project Preparation				○			
IN7	Using Statistics	◑	◑					●
IN8	Presenting Figures	◑	◑					●
IN9	Introduction to Information Technology	◑	◑					●
IN10	Computers and Communication Systems	◑	◑					●

* MCI M1 S Units of Competence

1. Maintain services and operations to meet quality standards
2. Contribute to the planning, monitoring and control of resources
3. Contribute to the provision of personnel
4. Contribute to the training and development of teams, individuals and self to enhance performance
5. Contribute to the planning, organization and evaluation of work
6. Create, maintain and enhance productive working relationships
7. Provide information and advice for action towards meeting organizational objectives

The chart indicates the Super Series 2 titles which provide some useful background information to support MCI M1 (Management level 1) Units of Competence.

Guide

NEBSM Super Series 2 Titles		MCI M1 Units of Competence (see below*)								
		1	2	3	4	5	6	7	8	9
PS1	Controlling Output	△	△							
PS2	Health and Safety	△								
PS3	Accident Prevention	△								
PS4	Ensuring Quality	△	△							
PS5	Quality Techniques	△	△							
PS6	Taking Decisions								△	△
PS7	Solving Problems		△						△	△
PS8	Productivity		△							
PS9	Stock Control Systems	△								
PS10	Stores Control	△								
PS11	Efficiency in the Office	△	△							
PS12	Marketing	△								
PS13	Caring for the Environment	△								
PS14	Caring for the Customer		△							
HR1	Supervising at Work							△		
HR2	Supervising with Authority							△		△
HR3	Team Leading					△	△	△		
HR4	Delegation					△	△	△		
HR5	Workteams					△	△	△		△
HR6	Motivating People							△		
HR7	Leading Change		△							
HR8	Personnel in Action					△				
HR9	Performance Appraisal							△		
HR10	Managing Time									
HR11	Hiring People					△				
HR12	Interviewing					△	△	△		
HR13	Training Plans					△				
HR14	Training Sessions					△				
HR15	Industrial Relations							△		
HR16	Employment and the Law				△			△		
HR17	Equality at Work				△			△		
HR18	Work-based Assessment					△	△			
FR1	Accounting for Money			△						
FR2	Control via Budgets			△						
FR3	Controlling Costs			△						
FR4	Pay Systems									
FR5	Security									
IN1	Communicating							△		△
IN2	Speaking Skills			△				△		△
IN3	Orders and Instructions							△		△
IN4	Meetings							△		△
IN5	Writing Skills			△			△	△		△
IN6	Project Preparation			△			△	△		
IN7	Using Statistics						△	△	△	
IN8	Presenting Figures						△	△		△
IN9	Introduction to Information Technology								△	△
IN10	Computers and Communication Systems								△	△

* MCI M1 Units of Competence

Key Role: Manage Operations
1. Maintain and improve service and product operations
2. Contribute to the implementation of change in services, products and systems

Key Role: Manage Finance
3. Recommend, monitor and control the use of resources

Key Role: Manage People
4. Contribute to the recruitment and selection of personnel
5. Develop teams, individuals and self to enhance performance
6. Plan, allocate and evaluate work carried out by teams, individuals and self
7. Create, maintain and enhance effective working relationships

Key Role: Manage Information
8. Seek, evaluate and organise information for action
9. Exchange information to solve problems and make decisions

Guide | Unit Completion Certificate

Completion of this Certificate by an authorized and qualified person indicates that you have worked through all parts of this unit and completed all assessments. If you are studying this unit as part of a certificated programme, or think you may wish to in future, then completion of this Certificate is particularly important as it may be used for exemptions, credit accumulation or Accreditation of Prior Learning (APL). Full details can be obtained from NEBSM.

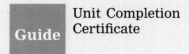

NEBSM
SUPER
SERIES
Second Edition

PS14

Caring for the Customer

....

has satisfactorily completed this unit.

Name of Signatory.............
Position.....................
Signature....................

Date........

Official Stamp

Keep in touch

Pergamon Open Learning and NEBS Management are always happy to hear of your experiences of using the Super Series to help improve supervisory and managerial effectiveness. This will assist us with continuous product improvement, and novel approaches and success stories may be included in promotional information to illustrate to others what can be done.

1   NEBSM Super Series 2 study links

Here are the Super Series 2 units which link to *Caring for the Customer*. You may find this useful when putting together your study programme but you should bear in mind that:

● each Super Series 2 unit stands alone and does not depend upon being used in conjunction with any other unit;

● Super Series 2 units can be used in any order which suits your learning needs.

ENSURING QUALITY Caring for the customer is very much a quality issue, and much of what this unit has to say is relevant, particularly the sections for dealing with systems for achieving quality.

MARKETING Caring for the customer is an aspect of marketing, since its main purpose is to help organizations hold on to their existing customers by satisfying their expectations. A marketing approach is very important for managers who are trying to achieve this.

QUALITY TECHNIQUES This unit is designed to help you recognize the role you can play in achieving quality goals and in employing some of the techniques used in the display and analysis of quality data.

CARING FOR THE CUSTOMER This unit covers the management aspects of customer service, focusing on the concept of 'total customer satisfaction'. It should enable you to take some practical steps to improving the quality of service which your team provides.

TEAM LEADING Good teamwork is fundamental to providing a high quality of service for the customer, and managers who wish to achieve this will need all the basic teamwork skills, especially the ability to communicate and motivate.

MOTIVATING PEOPLE Shows just what makes people want to work, the satisfaction gained from it and how to treat the workteam so as to achieve high performance and job satisfaction.

TRAINING PLANS No-one can deliver the right quality of care without the right level of competence. Improving standards of care will certainly involve reviewing skills, assessing training needs, and providing the training.

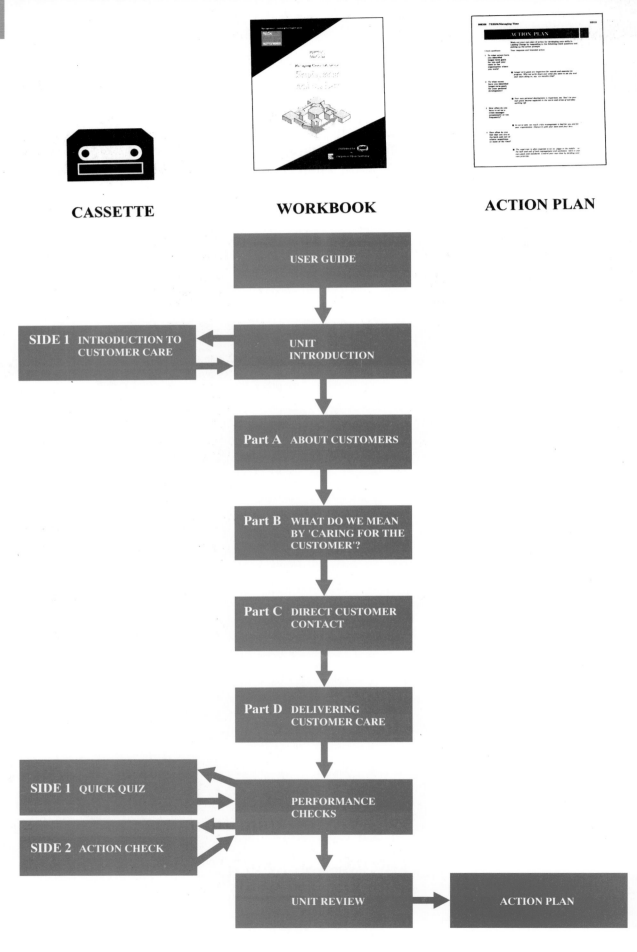

CASSETTE **WORKBOOK** **ACTION PLAN**

USER GUIDE

SIDE 1 INTRODUCTION TO CUSTOMER CARE → UNIT INTRODUCTION

Part A ABOUT CUSTOMERS

Part B WHAT DO WE MEAN BY 'CARING FOR THE CUSTOMER'?

Part C DIRECT CUSTOMER CONTACT

Part D DELIVERING CUSTOMER CARE

SIDE 1 QUICK QUIZ

SIDE 2 ACTION CHECK → PERFORMANCE CHECKS

UNIT REVIEW → ACTION PLAN

It is a highly competitive world, and every organization is under increasing pressure to offer its customers a better deal. Trouble lies in store for those which fail to do so.

Customer care is often thought of as the 'up-front' niceties offered to the customer in a situation of direct contact, but this is far from being the whole story. The modern-day aim of total customer satisfaction can only be achieved when every aspect of the organization's activities, from product design to customer information, and every single person, from the chief executive to the most lowly cleaner, is geared and committed to meeting the customer's needs.

All of this ultimately depends on people, and the performance of people depends on the quality of management.

Before you start work on this unit, listen carefully to Side one of the audio cassette, which sets the scene for your examination of *Caring for the Customer*.

SIDE 1

In this unit we will:

● define what is meant by a customer (both internal and external) and explain why we are all so dependent on our customers;

● examine the factors which contribute to customer satisfaction and consider what sort of service our customers expect from us;

● outline the role of supervisors and managers in delivering customer satisfaction;

● set out some practical steps which you can take to improve the quality of customer care which your team and organization provide.

Unit objectives

When you have worked through this unit you will ***be better able to***:

● explain the meaning and significance of customer care;

● identify your internal and external customers;

● identify your customers' expectations and any areas in which you are failing to meet them;

● provide an effective lead for your team in raising the standard of customer care which you provide;

● ensure that you and your team members perform to a high standard in customer contact situations.

ABOUT CUSTOMERS

1   Introduction

Before we decide how to 'care' for our customers, we need to establish who they are. This may not be as obvious as it seems. We will try to show that:

● a customer is not just someone who buys something from you;

● both commercial and non-commercial organizations have customers.

Our messages will be that:

● every organization needs to identify its external customers ;

● it should ensure that it is in the business of meeting their needs.

But we will also explain why everyone working inside an organization also has internal customers, whose needs also have to be met.

2   What is a customer?

Activity 1

■ Time guide 2 minutes

Try to say in *one* or *two* sentences what you think is meant by a 'customer'.

_____

_____

_____

A manager of a menswear shop would probably say that customers are the individuals who come into the shop to look at the goods, and perhaps to buy.

Someone working in the sales team of a manufacturing company probably thinks of customers as:

(a) the organizations which buy from the company;
(b) the individuals within them who make the purchasing decisions.

This is the *commercial* sector, and at this simple level, a customer is:

>   someone who buys our goods and services.

It is obvious that all the following have customers (though the solicitors and architects probably call them 'clients')

● retailers;

● travel agents;

● manufacturing firms;

● architects;

- wholesalers;
- bus companies;
- restaurants and hotels;
- firms of solicitors;
- car rental companies;
- building societies;
- insurance companies;
- haulage firms.

Anyone who works at the 'sharp end' of a commercial organization knows that customers are *extremely important*. Let's analyse why exactly this is.

Activity 2

■ Time guide 4 minutes

1. Suppose you need to travel to a town 100 miles away. Write down *half a dozen* different means by which you could make your journey.

_____

_____

_____

2. Suppose you decided that the best option was to hire a car. Write down the names of *three* or *four* firms from which you could do so.

_____

_____

Customers usually have plenty of choice when they buy goods and services. In this case, the possible means of transport include:

■ hitching a lift;

■ hiring a car;

■ taxi;

■ bus or coach;

■ using your own car;

■ rail.

You could walk or cycle, if you had enough time and energy, or perhaps even take a boat or a plane.

If you decided to hire a car, you would have the choice of national operators like Avis, Hertz and Budget, or a smaller local firm.

This is the 'market' at work:

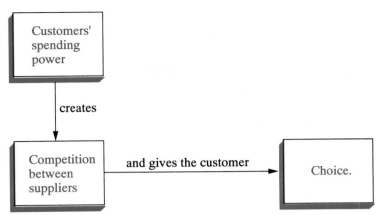

This has a colossal impact on commercial organizations. They are :

completely dependent

on *selling* their goods and services, and thus

completely dependent

on their *customers*.

In the commercial sector at least, customers not only have *choice*; they also have *power*. That's why so many organizations use the slogan:

the customer is king.

If customers don't like what a firm has to offer, they can simply choose another. If enough customers do this, they have the power to damage severely, and even destroy the organizations whose offer they reject.

Organizations which live by supplying goods and services to the market have *no choice* but to *compete* for customers: their survival depends on it. They also have to listen carefully to the 'messages' that customers send them when they make their choices.

When you choose to hire a car from Avis rather than Fred's Garage, you are sending Fred the message that something in his 'offer' is wrong, and that he is going to have to try harder next time.

Activity 3

■ Time guide 3 minutes

Can you think of any areas of business or commerce where there is little or no competition and customers have little or no choice? Try to write down *two* or *three* examples:

_____

_____

There are a few. Some public utilities, like electricity distribution and the water industry, are 'natural monopolies', irrespective of whether they are publicly or privately owned. British Telecom and British Rail are in a similar position, though there is a lot of pressure to open them up to competition.

Part A

Everyone pays lip service to 'the importance of competition', but many businesses would secretly prefer not to have any. Most countries, including the UK, find they have to pass laws to prevent big firms monopolizing their markets.

Even so, monopolies are not always a guarantee of commercial success, as this case study shows.

Sourpuss Ltd had a monopoly: they were the sole UK wholesale distributors to the retail trade of the fashionable Italian-made Fustanella brand of men's shirts. Although they made large profits, they were inefficient and unhelpful. Orders from retailers often went astray, invoices were incorrect, deliveries were cancelled or postponed without warning, and messages and inquiries were often lost or ignored.

Complaints to the sales reps resulted in no improvement, and eventually a group of their major retail customers decided to complain direct to the manufacturers.

Having checked for themselves, the Italian management promptly tore up their contract with Sourpuss and appointed a new distributor. Sourpuss lost three quarters of its business overnight and 20 of its 25 staff were made redundant.

The Managing Director sent each of the redundant staff a letter in which he blamed their inefficiency and poor attitude for the disaster – which in itself gives a clear indication of what was wrong in his company.

We can sum up the situation in the commercial sector by saying:

● many suppliers compete in the market;

● customers have plenty of choice;

● suppliers who fail to provide what their customers need are asking for trouble.

---

3   Non-commercial organizations and their customers

But what about non-commercial organizations? Don't they operate in a different way? Do they even have 'customers'?

Activity 4

■ Time guide 1 minute

Which of the following organizations would you say have 'customers'? Tick those that in your opinion do.

Boots ☐

the central library ☐

the county NHS hospital ☐

Glosser & Slant (public relations consultants) ☐

Rank Xerox Photocopier Division ☐

the Railway Hotel ☐

the local Further Education College ☐

British Steel ☐

the Probation Service ☐

There is no argument about the commercial organizations in the list: obviously they must have customers, because they are dependent on selling goods or services in the market. But what about the non-commercial organizations in the list?

■ The central library serves people who want to borrow books.

■ The county NHS hospital serves people who are ill.

■ The Further Education College serves its students, and to some extent their parents.

■ The Probation Service serves people who are in trouble with the law (like all social services, they refer to these people as 'clients').

These are publicly funded organizations whose services are mostly *free*. They do not have **paying customers**. They may not even think of the people who use their services as 'customers' at all.

Does this explain why there has been so much criticism of public services in recent years?

Activity 5

■ Time guide 1 minute

Tick any of these statements criticizing the quality of public services that you agree with:

1. 'People who work for these services just want an easy life: you can't expect them to put in as much effort as staff in the private sector do.' ☐

2. 'It's a matter of money: if we all had to pay for hospital care we would get a better service.' ☐

3. 'The public sector will never improve until there is competition and users have a choice.' ☐

4. 'The public sector doesn't care about efficiency because it knows the government will always bail it out.' ☐

We often hear statements like these, and may feel inclined to agree with them. Really they are all saying the same thing: that if the public sector operated like the private sector (that is, with suppliers competing for customers in a market), customer service would improve.

However, while there are seeds of truth in this, you would probably agree with me that:

■ many of the people in the non-commercial sector work extremely hard, while there are plenty of people in the commercial sector who don't;

■ plenty of commercial firms provide a poor service, even though it has to be paid for, while there are plenty of free public services which are excellent;

■ plenty of organizations give a poor service even though they are in a competitive market, while others where there is no competition give an excellent one;

■ the public sector can't always expect to be bailed out: inefficient units are likely to find themselves drastically reorganized, broken up or even closed down.

Let's sum up the differences between the commercial and non-commercial sectors on the question of customers.

The commercial sector:

● **depends directly on the customer** (nevertheless, we know from experience that many businesses **do not** provide good customer care).

The non-commercial public sector:

● does not necessarily think of the people who receive its services as 'customers';

● does not depend on them financially in such a direct way.

Perhaps the situation would be different if the users of these services had more choice, and thus became customers in the commercial sense? The State could perhaps achieve this by changing the ground-rules, for example:

● giving patients the right to register with whichever GP they choose;

● giving parents the right to choose which school their children attend;

● giving people vouchers with which to 'buy' housing, education, health care, or training services from the supplier of their choice.

According to this line of thinking, the ultimate goal would be an 'internal market', where each school, college, GP, hospital etc. would have to compete for customers in order to survive.

Activity 6

■ Time guide 5 minutes

Think about the way a hospital operates. What difference do you think it makes when a hospital regards the people it serves as customers rather than just as patients? Note down **two** or **three** ideas.

_____

_____

_____

The difference between a customer and a patient is that a customer expects a better service, and is in a position to **demand** it – that is, the consequences for the hospital and its staff of failing to meet the customer's needs will be significant.

This doesn't mean that a 'customer' can necessarily expect better **medical** treatment than a 'patient', but that he or she can expect to be treated better in other ways.

Take meals, for example. Traditionally, hospitals used to offer a very narrow choice of meals, which came at fixed times, usually much earlier than the patients would eat at home.

The attitude used to be that:

■ hospitals are a free service for which patients ought to be grateful;

■ so patients should be expected to fit in with the routines that suit the hospital and its staff.

When the hospital regards the patient as a customer, it has to start providing its services the way the customer wants, for example:

- a wider choice of meals;

- served at more civilized times.

Some hospital staff might argue that hospitals are places of healing, not hotels, but this is precisely the point. Every organization that wants to succeed must ask itself:

what business are we really in?

At one time, some hospitals used to answer this question by saying: 'our business is to treat illnesses, and if possible cure them.' This led to a 'culture' in which:

- doctors were interested only in diseases, and seldom bothered to explain anything to the patients;

- visiting hours were very restricted;

- the whole atmosphere was severe and forbidding;

- the facilities were minimal and the decor depressing.

Activity 7

> ■ **Time guide 3 minutes**
>
> Try to suggest a definition of 'what business a hospital is really in' that takes a wider view of the needs of the patient.
>
> _____
>
> _____
>
> _____

It is true that dealing with the patient's health problem is the most important issue, but I would say that hospitals are *in the business of meeting their customers' needs*, and that these needs include:

- 'hotel services', such as a friendly reception, a decent meal, a good night's sleep, comfort, lounges in which to read or watch TV, access to telephones etc.;

- proper information and advice about their condition – including counselling for people with serious or incurable conditions;

- the widest possible access for family and friends.

A visit to hospital used to be a rather intimidating experience, but now that hospitals have become more 'customer-friendly', a great deal has changed. Fewer doctors talk down to their patients; reception areas are warmer and more comfortable, with shops, cafes and children's playrooms. And visiting hours have become much more flexible.

This is much better for the customer, and any non-commercial organization can achieve similar improvements once it:

- starts thinking in terms of 'customers';

- asks itself what business it is really in;

- puts the customer's needs before its own.

Competition for cash may help, but for both commercial and non-commercial organizations, the keys to improving customer care are:

● *re-thinking the business*;

● *changing attitudes*.

Activity 8

■ Time guide 6 minutes

Local Authority planning departments are responsible for processing applications for planning permission from individuals and organizations in their area. The procedure is laid down by law, and the local Planning Officers are not obliged to do more than follow the rules.

At Gruffshire County Council, the Planning Department saw itself as 'in the business of processing planning applications', and its aim was to do so accurately and efficiently, according to the law. However, to applicants the Department appeared cold, bureaucratic and unhelpful.

The newly appointed Director of Planning Services proposed a change of approach:

■ identifying applicants as customers;

■ identifying the Department's business as 'helping customers to make successful applications for planning permission'.

She explained the advantages for applicants, but made it clear that she also believed that the change would be in the interests of the Department and its staff.

Given what we have said previously, what do you think the benefits to the Department and its staff might be? Try to suggest at least *two*:

_____

_____

_____

I think there are three important areas of benefit for the staff. See if you agree.

■ *Improved efficiency*: they will be able to iron out problems at an earlier stage, cutting the amount of paperwork and reducing the number of re-applications. This means a more efficient process and less frustration for staff and customers alike.

■ *More job-satisfaction*: the staff will have more contact with their customers and there will be fewer complaints. They will have a higher profile and receive more recognition for their work.

■ *More job security*: the department will be more popular with customers and with their representatives (the elected councillors). This may improve its chances of survival in a period when local government is under pressure to cut staff and contract out services to the private sector, though there is no guarantee of this.

Activity 9

■ Time guide 5 minutes

Try to apply these ideas to your own work situation.

What business is your organization in?

_____

_____

What are your customers' needs?

_____

_____

Whatever kind of organization you work for, it should be in the business of meeting its customers' needs; and you should have taken a broad view of these. Customers' needs go beyond the basic goods and services which you provide.

4   Some other external customers

It is *in the interests* of both commercial and non-commercial organizations to regard the people to whom they supply their services as customers, whether or not they are *paying* customers.

But are the shoppers, purchasing officers, patients, clients and applicants that we have looked at so far the *only* customers to consider?

Most organizations serve other groups of people as well. Here is an example:

Case Study

Organisation:

Icicle Frozen Foods plc (a chain of High Street frozen food shops).

It serves:

● *individual shoppers (consumers);*

● *the financial institutions which own 60 per cent of its shares;*

● *the Local Authority (to which it pays rates and which makes sure it obeys the consumer, planning and shop opening laws);*

● *the Environmental Health Department (which is responsible for enforcing food hygiene regulations);*

● *HM Customs and Excise (for VAT returns and because the shops also sell wines and spirits).*

It is in Icicle's interests to keep these various groups happy, and the best way to do this is to treat them as customers – that is, by giving them the kind of service and consideration that customers can expect.

Activity 10

■ Time guide 6 minutes

1. Jester Plastic Products Ltd is a smallish (60 employees) manufacturing firm. It produces injection-moulded plastic toys and components. It sells to the 'trade' only. The components are such things as saucepan handles, parts used in domestic electrical fittings, and various items for the vehicle manufacturing sector.

   Who would you say Jester Plastics should think of as customers, apart from its primary business customers?

   _____

   _____

   _____

   _____

2. Slough Council's Parks Department is responsible for several parks and playgrounds in the town. Its primary customers are the people who use these facilities. Who else do you think the Department might consider to be customers?

   _____

   _____

   _____

   _____

You may have thought of quite a few, but these are what I came up with:

1. Jester Plastic Products Ltd:

   ■ the shareholders (it may be independent or be wholly owned by some larger organization);

   ■ the Health and Safety Executive (which periodically inspects manufacturing premises for safety and investigates accidents);

   ■ the Local Authority, HM Customs and Excise (for the same sort of reasons that I gave for Icicle Frozen Foods plc);

   ■ the Inland Revenue (for NHI and PAYE returns).

   There might well be others, such as the local Training and Enterprise Council, if Jester takes work experience trainees.

   Jester's primary customers are businesses – 'the trade'. However, the ultimate buyers of its products are individual consumers. Firms like this must consider the needs of their *ultimate consumers* as well.

2. Slough Parks Department:

   ■ the local Council (which is responsible for the Department overall);

   ■ the local community generally;

   ■ the people who live near the parks.

I am not fully up-to-date with their activities, but Slough Parks Department used to be famous for their massed plantings of bedding flowers, and always had a large exhibition at the Chelsea Flower Show. This would suggest that passing motorists and flower lovers generally should also be included among their 'customers'.

5   Internal customers

So far we have looked at *external customers* – the various outsiders that organizations serve.

Now let's think about *internal customers*, and once again use a large hospital as an example.

Large hospitals exist to serve external customers (patients, their families, the Health Authorities etc.). Their main burden of service is carried by their 'front-line' departments:

● medical;

● genito-urinary;

● obstetrics and gynaecology;

● psychiatric;

● surgical;

● geriatric.

However, there are also various internal service departments whose job is to support the work of the front-line departments. Catering is an obvious example.

Activity 11

■ Time guide 3 minutes

What other internal services would you expect to find in a large general hospital? Try to list at least *six*.

_____

_____

_____

You probably listed at least some of these:

■ X-ray;

■ cleaning;

■ pharmacy;

■ counselling;

■ reception;

■ physiotherapy;

■ nursing;

■ maintenance;

■ pathology lab;

■ security;

■ nurse training;

■ boiler room.

15

Some of these departments – like reception, nursing and counselling – obviously have a front-line customer-contact role too; but their main purpose is to contribute to the work of the treatment departments.

We can map out this set of service relationships, showing internal customers with green arrows and external ones with black:

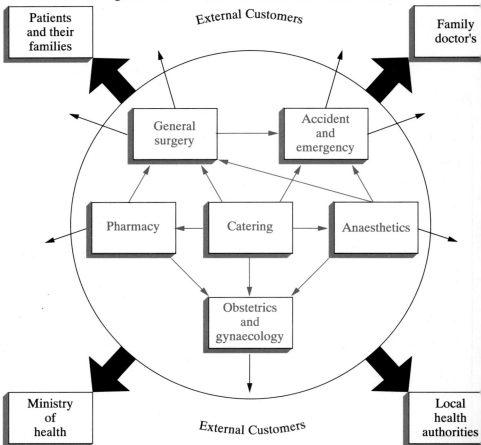

The real picture is even more complex, because there are many departments which we have not shown, including those concerned with management. However, the diagram clearly shows that there are plenty of internal as well as external customers here.

Activity 12

■ Time guide 2 minutes

Who would you say the X-ray Department's customers are?

_____

_____

_____

The Department serves both external customers:

■ the patients that other departments send to be X-rayed;

and internal customers:

■ the front-line medical and surgical departments that send the patients and need to see their X-rays;

■ the hospital management, which is responsible for ensuring that the hospital as a whole functions properly in the interests of its customers

Looked at this way, any sizeable organization consists of a complex network of customer–supplier relationships:

● the business of the hospital as a whole is to serve its external customers;

● the business of the front-line departments is to carry the main burden of customer service;

● the business of the second-line departments is to help them do so.

Commercial organizations have a system of internal customers too.

Activity 13

■ Time guide 8 minutes

RMB Technoline Ltd makes advanced testing equipment for use in the electronics industry. It sells both to industry and to higher education.

Most of the 180 staff work in one of the following functions:

■ Sales and Marketing;

■ Research and Development;

■ Production;

■ Stores;

■ Purchasing.

Draw up a diagram showing the internal and external customer relationships, in the same way as we did earlier for the large hospital.

Part A

My version of the diagram is on page 22. Don't look at it until you have finished working on your own.

Organizations are like complicated machines:

- all the different parts are connected;
- even the smallest parts play a vital role in making the machine work.

When one department isn't pulling its weight, the organization is like a bike with a missing pedal, or a car 'missing' on one cylinder.

In the race for competitive success, it will soon start falling behind, as this case study shows.

Benedorma was a Europe-wide hotel chain, catering for business travellers. It operated a central reservations system, based in Paris. Any customer could call Paris free of charge and book a room in any Benedorma hotel.

The staff in the reservations service were generally efficient and pleasant; so for the most part were the staff in the various hotels. Benedorma accepted reservations at very short notice, but customers who booked less than 24 hours ahead often found that there was no room for them when they arrived. This was because the hotel had not been notified of the reservation.

There were numerous complaints from customers, and hotel managers became very critical of the reservations system.
An inquiry found that the fault lay with the 'despatching' department which was responsible for passing reservations on to the hotels. The despatchers responded by saying that Benedorma did not offer an absolute guarantee of a room for someone booking within 24 hours of occupancy (which was technically true). Despatching staff worked a normal day shift and stopped work at 6 p.m. If they were particularly busy, some reservations would be left over until the next day, and it was the short-notice bookings among these which caused the problem.

Benedorma's answer to this customer care problem was:

1. to change its policy so that every accepted booking carried a guarantee that the room would be ready and waiting;

2. to retrain the despatching staff;

3. to change the despatching procedures so that short-notice reservations would be separated out for priority handling.

Finally let's consider your own position.

Activity 14

> ■ Time guide 6 minutes
>
> Think carefully about your own situation at work.
> 1. Who are your organization's external customers?
>
> _____
>
> _____
>
> _____
>
> *continued overleaf*

2. Even if you work in a front-line customer contact role, you will also have your own internal customers. Who are they?

_____

_____

_____

This will of course be different in every case, but your internal customers will certainly include:

■ the people to whom you report;

■ the people to whom you supply services;

■ the people who rely on your co-operation.

In every line of work, serving the external customers is the top priority.

And if you're not serving those customers, you'd better be serving someone who is!

Self check 1

■ Time guide 15 minutes

1. Fill in the blanks in these sentences so that they make sense.

   (a) Our customers are the people whom we _____, whether they are _____ or _____ our organization, and whether they _____ for our services or not.

   (b) In the commercial sector, customers' _____ power creates _____, which gives customers _____.

   (c) Every organization needs to think carefully about what _____ it is really in.

2. Explain briefly why it is useful to regard your own management team as 'customers'.

   _____

   _____

   _____

continued overleaf

3. Draw up a customer–supplier diagram showing the internal and external relationships which exist in a prison. You may want to draft this out on scrap paper before putting your considered version below.

Include the following:

■ the Home Office;

■ the courts;

■ the local community;

■ prisoners;

■ prisoners' families;

■ warders;

■ the Governor's office;

■ the administration office;

■ the catering service.

Response check 1

1. (a) Our customers are the people whom we SERVE, whether they are INSIDE or OUTSIDE our organization, and whether they PAY for our services or not.

   (b) In the commercial sector, customers' SPENDING power creates COMPETITION, which gives customers CHOICE.

   (c) Every organization needs to think carefully about what BUSINESS it is really in.

2. It is useful to regard your own management team as 'customers' because:

(a) you serve management, and they rely on the service which you provide;

(b) they have power over you, and it is in your interests to serve them well.

3.

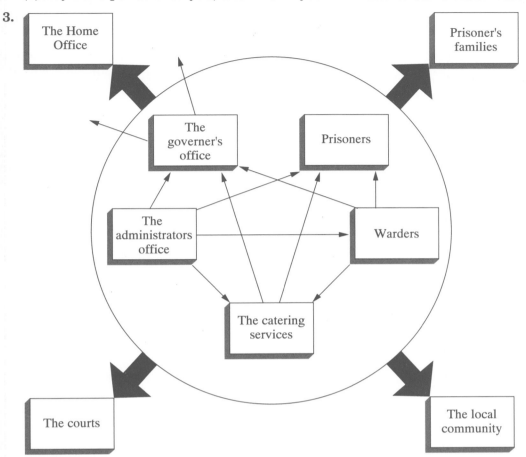

Although prisoners are there against their will, there is a strong argument for seeing them as customers, in the same way as a hotel sees its guests. Prisons are in the business of holding prisoners on behalf of the community generally, but in a way which minimizes conflict and discontent. People in the local community are also customers, because the prison has to help them feel comfortable about the fact that they have large numbers of convicted criminals living very close by.

6   Summary

- Both commercial and non-commercial organizations have customers.
- Customers are the people whom we serve, whether they pay for our services or not.
- Commercial organizations need to provide good service because they depend directly on competing for their customers' spending power.
- Non-commercial organizations also stand to benefit from providing good service – more efficiency, more job satisfaction, more job security.

● Everyone has customers:

   – organizations have external customers;

   – departments and individuals have internal customers as well.

● If internal suppliers aren't serving their internal customers properly, the external customers won't be served properly either.

● Not everyone is in the front line of customer service – but if you aren't serving customers yourself, you should be serving someone who is.

RMB Technoline Ltd.
Internal and external customer relations (from page 18).

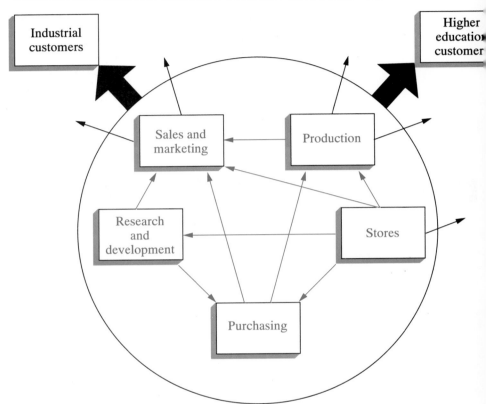

In this diagram, Purchasing serves all the other internal departments. Stores has an 'external customer' arrow because it supplies spare parts direct to customers. All the internal departments serve the front-line customer contact departments, Production and Sales and Marketing.

1   Introduction

Customer care is often misunderstood. People tend to assume that:

● it is all about being courteous and friendly to customers;

● only customer contact staff need to bother about it.

This is quite wrong: customer contact is an important area (which we will look at in Part C), but polite smiles are not the customer's top priority.

Customer care is part of marketing, and it plays a crucial part in ensuring the success of any organization. Unless it covers every aspect of the service provided to customers, starting with the product itself, it will not work.

2   Customers old and new

We can define customer care as

> serving the customer the way the customer expects to be served

and

> doing the things you need to do to keep your existing customers happy.

This is not the same as winning new customers, though many commercial firms devote a great deal of time and energy to doing this, through their sales and marketing activities.

Case Study

McGibbons is a pharmaceutical company which makes and sells drugs used for treating severe asthma. Its primary customers are family doctors and hospital specialists, because these have the authority to prescribe drugs and can opt for McGibbons' drugs rather than those of a competitor.

Out of McGibbons' 520 staff, 100 are employed in some aspect of sales or marketing.

The Marketing department consists of 20 people. They are responsible for working out strategy and controlling the annual advertising and promotion spend of £6,000,000.

The Sales department includes 40 'reps' who spend most of their time on the road visiting the primary customers.

The remaining 40 sales and marketing staff are involved in various sales support activities.

Activity 15

■ Time guide 3 minutes

From what you know of reps and selling, what would you say the main tasks of McGibbons' reps are?

_____

_____

_____

If they are like most sales reps, they will have three main tasks on their agenda:

■ identifying potential new customers and trying to win them;

■ keeping existing customers happy;

■ trying to sell new products to existing customers.

Anyone in this line of work will tell you that the first of these is extremely difficult. It is also expensive.

It costs McGibbons £35,000 a year to keep a rep and her car on the road. They reckon that each rep spends about a quarter of her time trying to win new customers, and that the average number of new customers won per rep per year is 20. This is a cost of £35,000 ÷ 4 ÷ 20 = £437.50. (The true cost per net new customer is higher, because each rep loses a few customers for various reasons.)

McGibbons also considers that £1.6 million of the advertising and promotion budget should be allocated to the winning of new customers. £1.6 million ÷ 20 ÷ 40 (the number of reps) = £2,000. So the total cost per new customer won is a staggering £2,437.50!

In many industries like insurance, banking and retailing a new customer costs less than this, but there are also sectors like defence, avionics, mainframe computing and heavy engineering where the customers are few but their purchasing power huge. In these sectors, the cost of winning a new customer can be very high.

Activity 16

■ Time guide 5 minutes

Sales people are in constant direct contact with their customers. Suppose you are such a customer – responsible for purchasing building materials for a local council's building maintenance department, for example. You will have a number of regular suppliers, and you will deal with their reps.

What would these reps need to do to keep you, as the customer, happy? (If you don't work in this kind of role, why not consult a colleague who does, before you answer?)

_____

_____

_____

_____

_____

_____

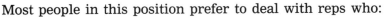

Most people in this position prefer to deal with reps who:

■ know their products thoroughly and can give reliable advice;

■ are pleasant to deal with (friendly, but not over-friendly);

■ are efficient (businesslike but not pushy);

■ are honest and truthful;

■ listen to customers and act on their wishes;

■ give the impression that customers are their top priority.

And every successful rep knows that keeping an existing customer is

ten times easier

and

ten times cheaper

than winning a new customer to replace one you have lost.

Unfortunately, many organizations have not yet discovered this important truth. They wrongly believe that:

● customer care is about slick sales people, sweet smiles and saying 'Have a nice day';

● customer care is solely the concern of the customer contact staff.

Certainly, skilful sales staff and 'personal niceties' help, but on their own they are **not enough**, as this case study shows.

X hired a TV and video from Rentquick Ltd. After some months, the TV broke down. X phoned Rentquick (who were very pleasant and helpful), and the following day an electrician arrived – a local tradesman who worked for them on a contract basis. He made a repair on the spot.

A week or so later, the same fault recurred, and once again X phoned Rentquick. This time the electrician did not arrive for three days, and he made the same repair as before. The TV failed again the following day, and X rang Rentquick to complain. They were very apologetic – and promised immediate action, but days passed and no electrician came.

X checked his rental contract, which stated that if any fault was not corrected within ten days of being reported, he could cancel the contract, and Rentquick would remove the equipment and refund the rental payments for the period when the equipment was out of order.

X wrote to Rentquick's Managing Director, explaining the situation and insisting on his contractual rights to cancellation and refund. The MD wrote a very apologetic letter back, in which he agreed to X's requests and promised to do better next time, if the chance ever arose. Shortly after, X received a similar letter from the Customer Services Manager, and a day or two later a van arrived and removed the TV and video.

A few days later, X received a letter from the Accounts Department at Rentquick, containing his refund cheque. However, in the same post came a new paying-in book, and a note asking him to 'use it in future'. This irritated X greatly (he had always paid by bank debit), but when a few days later he received another letter demanding an 'overdue' payment, he was absolutely furious.

X wrote to the MD again, pointing all this out, and saying what a useful case study it would make for the training course on customer service that he was about to write! And after that, the saga really did end.

Activity 17

■ Time guide 6 minutes

The people working for Rentquick did some things which were right, and others which were wrong. Read through the case study again carefully, and list all the points you can identify.

Done right:

_____

_____

_____

Done wrong:

_____

_____

_____

_____

_____

_____

Rentquick's staff were unfailingly polite, helpful and calm, and their senior managers replied to X's letters promptly and correctly. These are important points in their favour.

On the other hand, the service they actually delivered was very poor:

■ they supplied a faulty TV;

■ their electrician (who was not a direct employee) failed to fix the TV properly;

■ it was then left unrepaired for a long period;

■ communications between Customer Relations and Accounts broke down;

■ Accounts failed to understand the messages they were given;

■ and also failed to act on them;

■ the computer system was allowed to send out a final demand when it should not have done so;

■ staff made promises of service that they did not keep.

When this sort of thing happens, there is a tendency to blame the system or the computer, but the responsibility actually lies with the human beings in charge of the various stages of the system. The sales and marketing people won a customer. The sales support, customer service and accounts people lost him.

Activity 18

■ Time guide 4 minutes

This episode was bad news for Rentquick in *three* important respects. Think about the situation, and see if you can define what they are:

1. _____

2. _____

3. _____

First, they lost a customer, lost turnover and lost profit.

Second, the episode took up a large amount of staff time right up to Managing Director level (and time is money).

Third, their reputation was damaged.

A damaged reputation is no joke. Research has shown that:

● a *satisfied customer* tends to tell about four other people;

● a *dissatisfied* one tends to tell ten or more.

It is very easy to get a bad reputation for service, and very hard to get a good one.

3   The three pillars of customer satisfaction

It is the task of every organization to provide its customers with:

● the right product;

● at the right place;

● at the right time;

● at the right price (in the case of free public services this is the amount that taxpayers have to contribute to keep the service going);

● in the right way.

Note that we are using the word 'product' in a technical sense to mean whatever the particular organization supplies, whether this is goods, services, or a mixture of the two:

● Cadbury's product is   chocolates;

● a school's product is   education for children;

● Carpetland's product is   carpets and fitting services;

● a doctor's product is   diagnosis and treatment of illnesses;

● Powergen's product is   electricity;

● a police force's product is   protection against crime

The Rentquick case study shows that the 'personal niceties' side of customer care is far from being the crucial factor in satisfying – and therefore keeping – customers. Customer care is about getting the package we offer the customer right *as a whole*.

So what are the other factors involved? Let's start by considering an ordinary consumer.

Neville wanted a new front door for his house, and within half an hour's drive of where he lived there were eight firms where he could buy one:

- *B&Q;*
- *Sainsbury's Homebase;*
- *Magnet & Southern's;*
- *Texas Homecare;*
- *Great Mills;*
- *Just Doors Ltd (a local firm)*
- *Do It All*
- *Wickes.*

There is plenty of choice, and Neville has been a customer of all eight at some time or other. How does he decide which to go to this time? His decision will probably be based on weighing up a number of factors.

Activity 19

■ Time guide 4 minutes

There are many factors which might influence Neville's decision. List as many as you can think of:

_____

_____

_____

_____

_____

_____

Everyone has experience of this kind of shopping, so I expect you agree with me that these are the main questions that Neville might ask himself:

■ Do they stock the style of door I want?

■ Have they got a reasonable selection in stock?

■ How competitive is the price?

■ How good is the quality?

■ How near is the store?

■ How crowded will it be?

■ How close can I park?

■ Will they be open at the time I want to go?

■ Do they take Access?

■ Do the staff know their stuff?

■ Are they pleasant and helpful?

■ If there turns out to be a problem with the door after I have bought it, what will their attitude be?

Activity 20

■ Time guide 6 minutes

We can group all these 'satisfaction factors' under the three headings below. Try doing so yourself.

Product factors (the right product at the right price):

_____

_____

_____

_____

Convenience factors (at the right place at the right time):

_____

_____

_____

_____

Human factors (in the right way):

_____

_____

_____

_____

I would group them like this:

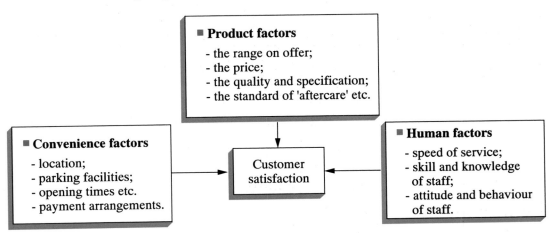

■ **Product factors**
- the range on offer;
- the price;
- the quality and specification;
- the standard of 'aftercare' etc.

■ **Convenience factors**
- location;
- parking facilities;
- opening times etc.
- payment arrangements.

Customer satisfaction

■ **Human factors**
- speed of service;
- skill and knowledge of staff;
- attitude and behaviour of staff.

If Neville had the time, he could compare the various suppliers using a table in which he gave each one a score out of five on each factor.

Satisfaction factors	Retail outlet 1	Retail outlet 2	Retail outlet 3	etc.
Range on offer	5	4	4	
Price	4	4	5	
Quality and specification	4	3	3	
etc.				

Activity 21

■ Time guide 2 minutes

Which of these three pillars of customer satisfaction is the most important? Explain why you think so.

The product factors.

The convenience factors.

The human factors.

It depends to some extent on the situation. For example:

■ if the product and the price are not right, it scarcely matters whether the staff are nice or nasty;

■ if the price is a real bargain, customers may put up with a lot of inconvenience;

■ if the product is widely available at the same price everywhere, the human factor may be very important indeed.

But what both private and commercial customers want above all from the goods or services supplied to them is:

complete reliability

and

no surprises.

This means that in a customer care programme the product factors usually come first and the human factors last. All the friendly smiles and polite greetings in the world will not compensate for unreliable goods or sub-standard services.

Now let's consider a commercial situation and see what satisfaction factors apply there.

Part B

Activity 22

■ **Time guide 4 minutes**

Tom is a supervisor with a major DIY retailer. He deals with two suppliers of doors – Woodhull Ltd and Claflin Ltd. They both provide the same product specification, price and quality, so product factors are not an issue.

Which other satisfaction factors do you think Tom, as a customer of these two firms, would judge them on?

Convenience factors: _____

_____

_____

_____

Human factors: _____

_____

_____

_____

I think that the key issues would probably be:

1. Convenience factors:

■ the flexibility of the service

  – can they change delivery schedules if need be?
  – can they deliver unscheduled requirements at short notice if need be?
  – are they willing to take back surplus stocks?

1. Human factors:

■ the efficiency of the staff

  – do they act promptly?
  – do they pass on messages?
  – do they get things right?
  – do deliveries arrive when promised?
  – do they match the order properly?

■ the personal qualities of the staff

  – are they friendly?
  – are they helpful?
  – do they make an effort to get things right?

These are all things which a paying customer like Tom would expect the suppliers to get right – but the product factors must be right first.

The customer does not expect the delivery lorries to be all walnut veneer and leather upholstery, or the drivers to be wearing business suits. The expectation is for a reasonably efficient service from reasonably presentable people – exactly the same as your customers expect from you.

31

In general, customers expect a service which is reasonably efficient, flexible and helpful, considering the circumstances, the price being paid, and the state of the trade.

Activity 23

■ Time guide 8 minutes

If you do not work in a direct customer contact role, you may need to consult colleagues who do in order to complete this activity.

1. Write down the main product (goods or services) which your organization supplies (choose just one of them, if there are several):

_____

2. Who are your main competitors in supplying this product?

_____

_____

3. What does your organization have to offer that your competitors do not?

_____

_____

_____

Perhaps you found it difficult to answer these questions. Indeed:

■ perhaps no-one has ever bothered to ask what your organization's customers expect;

■ perhaps you have no competitors, because you have a monopoly, or because you work in a public service which is not subject to direct competition;

■ perhaps there is nothing to choose between your organization and its various competitors.

Nevertheless, these are crucial questions which you, as a supervisor, must be able to answer if you are to play a full role in satisfying your customers, both internal and external.

The problem is that customers don't necessarily tell you whether they are satisfied or dissatisfied. They just take their business elsewhere.

Activity 24

■ Time guide 5 minutes

How can you tell whether your organization is satisfying its customers' expectations?
(Again, you may need to consult colleagues about this.)

_____

_____

_____

The best organizations are keenly interested in what their customers
think of them. If your own organization is one of these it will:

■ keep a careful log of complaints;

■ listen carefully to reports from the customer contact staff;

■ study the level of sales or customer throughput, and compare this
with how its competitors are doing.

If complaints are increasing, sales are falling and the
customer-contact staff are increasingly harassed, then this strongly
suggests that customers' expectations are not being met.

Activity 25

■ Time guide 5 minutes

You yourself may well be conscious of areas where dissatisfaction is high, or rising. Make a
brief note of the problem areas now, and whether they relate to product, convenience or
human factors.

External customer dissatisfaction: _____

_____

_____

Internal customer dissatisfaction: _____

_____

_____

It is important to *listen for dissatisfaction*, and the earlier this is
done, the better. This means:

1. *finding out what customers expect*;

2. *finding out how well you are satisfying these expectations*;

3. *taking action to bridge the 'expectation gap'*.

We will return to this topic in Part D, 'Delivering customer care'.

33

4.1
How much satisfaction should you give?

Case Study

Question one: Should you provide less than the customer expects, if you can get away with it?

Customer care costs money and effort, but if your standards of performance slide, you will soon be in trouble, even if you have little competition to worry about.

Custer & Bighorn specialised in short runs of metal carcases for the electrical industry. Among their customers was Slotworks Ltd., a company which made vending machines. Slotworks made roughly 50 Soupstar Mark 3 machines monthly, using C & B carcases. It wasn't a large order, but it was regular, and the two firms had negotiated an arrangement that suited them. C & B absorbed the large initial cost of setting up the complicated jigs and patterns for the carcases, in return for an understanding that there would continue to be regular orders provided things went well.

At first, C & B provided a satisfactory service, but gradually they came to take the Slotworks order for granted:

● *the sales manager stopped making courtesy calls;*

● *the production planners would often downgrade the Slotworks job if there was another urgent order in the factory ('It's all right, we'll put the Slotworks job back a couple of days.')*

● *the production foreman let the quality standards slide ('It's all right, Slotworks aren't that fussy')*

● *the delivery people became careless about handling and delivery times ('Chuck that on the bottom, it's only for Slotworks, we'll go there last.')*

Everyone at C & B was confident that they had got Slotworks 'over a barrel':

(a) they had the jigs and patterns for making the carcases, and it would take about three months before any other supplier could replicate them;

(b) if they delivered late, there was nothing that Slotworks could do about it;

(c) in any case the price was good;

(d) and there was an 'understanding' between the two firms.

On several occasions Slotworks had to reschedule production because deliveries from C & B came in late, or the quality was poor.

Activity 26

■ Time guide 3 minutes

Put yourself in the position of a production supervisor at Slotworks. There is only one supplier of these carcases but you are increasingly dissatisfied with the service C & B is providing. What can you do about it?

_____

_____

Slotworks pays its bills and is entitled to expect a reasonable service. If C & B won't provide it, there must be someone else who can.

I think that its first move would be to give C & B a 'rocket'. This usually improves things for a time, but C & B sounds like an outfit which doesn't understand the basics of customer care. So Slotworks will probably seek out a new supplier, even if this takes months to achieve.

Customers whose expectations are not met will always go elsewhere if they can.

Question two: Should you provide exactly what the customer wants, and no more?

Or should you provide them with more than they expect?

It is always useful to give your customers *a little more* than they expect, especially if this is in the area of human factors, which cost little or nothing. They will be impressed, and you will be more likely to keep them.

There is usually nothing to be gained from giving customers *substantially more* than they expect, though sometimes you can't avoid doing so.

Activity 27

■ Time guide 2 minutes

In what circumstances would you have to consider giving your customers substantially more than they have expected in the past?

If your competitors improve their 'offer', you can't afford to be left behind.

Consider the motor manufacturing business. Competition is fierce and each manufacturer tries to gain a competitive edge by offering not only high discounts but also material improvements to the product, such as:

● new features;

● higher specifications;

● six-year anti-corrosion guarantees;

● free servicing for a year;

● interest-free loans;

● free membership of AA or RAC.

In other sectors, suppliers compete to keep their customers happy by offering:

● free trial periods (for example office equipment suppliers);

● unconditional replacement of any item if faults appear (for example domestic appliances);

● a guarantee of an operation within two years (health authorities);

● the right to watch the work being done (for example vehicle servicing);

● the personal attention of a customer advisor (for example building societies);

● 'perks' such as 'loyalty' discounts, bonuses, free gifts, special offers and free competitions.

The danger in all this frenzied competition is that customers may come to expect more than the suppliers can afford to give them!

Activity 28

■ Time guide 2 minutes

We have clearly moved into the sphere of marketing. What would you say is the difference between customer care and marketing?

_____

_____

Marketing is about identifying and satisfying the needs of the customer in a way that meets the needs of the supplier (the need being to make a profit, to grow, or to survive in a healthy condition, etc.).

The marketing approach covers everything from the design of the product to the way it is delivered. It is concerned both with winning new customers and retaining old ones.

Customer care is part of the marketing approach – its purpose is to retain existing customers by satisfying their expectations.

Activity 29

■ Time guide 4 minutes

Trevor is a clerk in the Housing Benefit Office of Flatwick District Council. His job is to process new applications for benefit. When he has finished with each application he sends it on to another department. He has occasionally spoken to an external customer (a benefit applicant) on the phone, but has never met one face to face.

The Office wants to improve the standard of customer care in relation to its external customers (the benefit claimants). What significance do you think this has for Trevor?

_____

_____

The Office as a whole has many external customers, and some staff have a lot of direct contact with them. Trevor's position is different but he does play an important part in caring for the customer by ensuring that he:

■ processes the applications speedily and accurately;

■ notes any points which might need to be queried with the customer.

Customers expect an efficient and reliable service, and simply by doing his job **conscientiously** Trevor can improve the standard of customer care.

This applies equally to Trevor's internal customers:

● the department to which he sends the processed applications;

● management;

● colleagues in his own section who rely on him pulling his weight.

Activity 30

■ Time guide 6 minutes

Who is your own most important customer? (This may be an internal or external customer.)

_____

What does this customer expect from you and your team?

_____

_____

How well do you meet these expectations under the main customer satisfaction headings?
(Ring the statement which is nearest the truth.)

■ Product factors:

1	2	3	4	5
very well	quite well	so-so	not very well	very badly

■ convenience factors:

1	2	3	4	5
very well	quite well	so-so	not very well	very badly

■ human factors:

1	2	3	4	5
very well	quite well	so-so	not very well	very badly

Think carefully about your answers:

● customers' expectations may be higher than you think they are;

● you may not be meeting them as well as you think you are.

And in case anyone in your team still feels that internal customers aren't really important, remind them that:

● your organization depends on how well it serves its external customers;

● if you aren't serving them, you are certainly serving the people who are!

Self check 2

■ Time guide 2 minutes

1. Complete the following sentences so that they make sense:

(a) Customer care is serving the customer the way the customer _____ _____ _____ _____.

(b) It means doing the things you need to do to keep your _____ _____ happy.

continued overleaf

2. Are the following statements true or false?

    (a) If your organization loses customers it can always replace them. TRUE/FALSE

    (b) Customer care is mainly about the quality of the customer contact staff. TRUE/FALSE

    (c) The product factors are the most important element in customer satisfaction. TRUE/FALSE

    (d) Customers who are unhappy with your service can be expected to complain. TRUE/FALSE

    (e) Caring for customers and marketing are separate issues. TRUE/FALSE

3. On a typical day, Smollets upset three customers but pleased seven. Will their reputation be rising or falling?

4. Unscramble the words in brackets to show what customers want above all from the services supplied to them:

    ■ complete (IRA BITE LILY) _____

    ■ no (RUSS'S PIER) _____

5. Why is it good policy to give customers a little more than they expect?

    _____

    _____

6. Complete these two sentences so that they make sense.

    (a) Customers' _____ may be higher than you _____ .

    (b) You may not be _____ them as _____ as you think you are.

Response check 2

1. (a) Customer care is serving the customer the way the customer EXPECTS TO BE SERVED.

    (b) It means doing the things you need to do to keep your EXISTING CUSTOMERS HAPPY.

2. (a) If your organization loses customers it can always replace them. This statement is TRUE, but it is much more expensive and difficult to win new customers than to keep existing ones.

    (b) Customer care is mainly about the quality of the customer contact staff. This is FALSE. Everyone in an organization contributes to the quality of the service it provides, and those who do not have direct contact with external customers should still be serving the others who do.

    (c) The product factors are the most important element in customer satisfaction. This is TRUE, though once the product is right the other factors become more significant.

    (d) Customers who are unhappy with your service can be expected to complain. This is FALSE. In Britain at least, customers who are upset tend not to complain but to 'vote with their feet'.

    (e) Caring for customers and marketing are separate issues. This is FALSE. Customer care is part of the marketing approach.

3. On a typical day, Smollets upset three customers but pleased seven. On balance, their reputation will be FALLING. Dissatisfied customers tend to tell about ten other people, while satisfied ones tell only about four. The calculation here is:

	Customers	People told per customer	Total of people told
Dissatisfied	3	10	30
Satisfied	7	4	28

4.

■ complete RELIABILITY;

■ no SURPRISES.

5. It is good policy to give customers a little more than they expect because they will be impressed, and you will be more likely to keep them.

6. (a) Customers' EXPECTATIONS may be higher than you THINK.

(b) You may not be MEETING them as WELL as you think you are.

5 Summary

- Customer care is part of marketing. Its aim is:
  - to keep existing customers happy;
  - by serving them the way they expect to be served.

- It is ten times easier and ten times cheaper to keep an existing customer satisfied than to win a new one.

- Every aspect of the service you provide plays a part in customer satisfaction under one of these headings:
  - product factors (the right product at the right price);
  - convenience factors (at the right place and time);
  - human factors (in the right way).

- Dissatisfied customers do not always complain, but they will tell other people and will take their business elsewhere if they can.

- It is important to listen for dissatisfaction and to deal with the problem early:
  - by monitoring complaints;
  - asking customers' opinions.

- The aim should be to provide the service that customers expect, and if possible a little more.

- It is the service as a whole which creates customer satisfaction, and everyone in an organization contributes to that service in some way.

- If you're not serving customers yourself, make sure you provide the right service for the people who do.

DIRECT CUSTOMER CONTACT

Part
C

1 Introduction

Everyone tends to assume that customer contact is the most important part of customer care, but it isn't.

Of course, the way we deal person-to-person with our customers *is* important. It's just that it is more important to be able to provide the right product at the right price at the right time in the right place. When you've got all that right, it's time to start concentrating on the personal issues.

In Part B we made the point that, although some staff are specifically responsible for customer contact (receptionists, sales people, customer order staff etc.), virtually everyone has direct contact with their customers at some time or other.

This is even more true of internal customers than of external ones, which is why we believe that *all* staff need to develop basic customer contact skills.

In Part C we will look at customer contact as it takes place:

● on the telephone;

● face-to-face.

and will suggest some standard guidelines for quality customer contact which you and your workteam can follow. We will also deal with the difficult matter of customer complaints.

2 Whose customers are they?

Many people think that the responsibility for customer care lies with those staff who are employed specifically in customer contact roles.

Activity 31

■ Time guide 3 minutes

Who would you say were the customer contact staff in:

a branch of W H Smiths: _____

a hospital: _____

the local social security office: _____

a building society: _____

a car manufacturing firm: _____

a large hotel: _____

All of these have staff whose specific role is to be in direct contact with customers. In shops it is the sales staff; in hospitals it is receptionists, nurses, surgeons, physiotherapists, radiographers, pharmacists and various others; in the social security office and the building society it is the counter staff and to some extent the manager; in the car manufacturing firm it is the sales force and the customer support and liaison teams; in big hotels it is receptionists, porters, bar staff, waiters, security staff and garage attendants.

These people are in the front line, but that doesn't mean they are the only ones responsible for customer care.

Activity 32

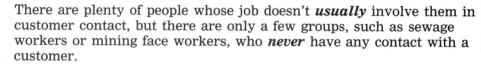

■ Time guide 2 minutes

Try to think of people in your own organization who *never* have any contact with the organization's external customers. Note down the work that they do.

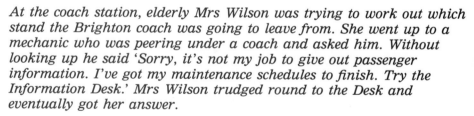

There are plenty of people whose job doesn't *usually* involve them in customer contact, but there are only a few groups, such as sewage workers or mining face workers, who *never* have any contact with a customer.

Here is an example:

Case
Study

At the coach station, elderly Mrs Wilson was trying to work out which stand the Brighton coach was going to leave from. She went up to a mechanic who was peering under a coach and asked him. Without looking up he said 'Sorry, it's not my job to give out passenger information. I've got my maintenance schedules to finish. Try the Information Desk.' Mrs Wilson trudged round to the Desk and eventually got her answer.

There was probably nothing in the mechanic's job description about 'providing enquirers with accurate information about coach services'. If tackled about it, he would probably say 'My job is to make sure the coaches are roadworthy and customers are none of my business.'

Maintenance is an important job, which also serves the customers' needs. But just once he did meet a customer – and promptly made a mess of it. After that, even if everyone else was charming and helpful, Mrs Wilson will probably think twice before travelling by coach again.

All staff who *may* come into contact with customer should be trained to treat them the right way.

3.1
The ABC of service

It should be obvious what customers expect from their suppliers' staff; we are all customers ourselves, and we know what good service and bad service mean.

The quality of customer service depends entirely on human factors. These can be summed up in the ABC of customer service:

A ttitude;
B ehaviour;
C ompetence.

Activity 33

■ Time guide 5 minutes

Think of a recent situation where you – as a private customer – received **good** service, and another where you received **poor** or **bad** service. Describe briefly what happened in each case.

1. Good service: _____

_____

_____

2. Bad service: _____

_____

_____

Here are three examples from my personal experience:

1. Good service: I had to hire a car, but wasn't able to collect it during the hirer's normal working hours. 'No problem sir,' said the manager, 'I'll bring it out to you myself.' This involved good *attitude* (being willing to do that little bit extra to help) and good *behaviour* (being friendly and polite).

2. Bad service: I wanted to buy a particular technical book. I went to the desk to ask a sales assistant, but she seemed to be very busy doing something else, and didn't even look at me. After a few moments I said 'Excuse me...', but, still without looking up, she said 'Sorry, I'm busy. You'll have to ask someone else.' This involved bad *attitude* (not being willing to help) and bad *behaviour* (an unfriendly manner and failure to look me in the eye).

3. Good service: I phoned my computer suppliers to ask about a problem I was having with a disk drive. The person who answered my call said, 'I'm sorry, sir, I'm not familiar with that particular machine, and the person who deals with it is tied up at the moment. If you'll give me your name and phone number, I'll explain what the problem is and ask her to get back to you as soon as she's free.' Half an hour later, the other person called back and sorted out my problem.

That was an example of all three elements of the ABC at work: good *attitude*, good *behaviour* and *competence* (from the person who competently passed on my message and the one who competently solved my problem).

The basis of a good attitude to customer care is accepting that:

● customers are the most important people in our working life;

● satisfying their needs is our most important task.

We need to respect our customers – which means meeting their needs in a way which is friendly and accessible, without becoming too 'familiar'. Supervisors should constantly remind their teams of these ideas, and make sure they provide a consistent example for the team members to follow.

• When team members accept that customers are the most important people:	→ then it makes sense to do that little bit extra to help them.
• When team members accept that satisfying customers' needs is the most important task:	→ then it makes sense to give serving customers priority over all their other tasks.

Activity 34

■ Time guide 7 minutes

Answer this short questionnaire on behalf of your workteam. Your answers should be a true representation of the general attitude of the members of the team.

	Always true	Sometimes true	Never true
1. We think of the people we supply as customers, whether they are inside or outside the organization.	☐	☐	☐
2. The individual members of the team are happy to deal with customers, even if that isn't their specific role.	☐	☐	☐
3. All the team members clearly understand that our jobs depend on how well we serve our customers' needs.	☐	☐	☐
4. We put meeting customers' needs before all other considerations.	☐	☐	☐
5. The individual members of the team are willing to make an extra effort to help a customer.	☐	☐	☐
6. We are friendly and helpful to customers, even if things aren't going well.	☐	☐	☐

continued overleaf

7. We do not argue with customers, or get irritable with them.

☐   ☐   ☐

8. Team members are willing to help each other provide a better service.

☐   ☐   ☐

9. If we fail to satisfy our customers, we try to establish what went wrong and find ways of ensuring it doesn't happen again.

☐   ☐   ☐

10. We discuss the quality of our service, and try to keep one step ahead of what our customers expect .

☐   ☐   ☐

Score two points for each answer in the 'always true' column; one point for 'sometimes true' and zero for 'never true', and add up the total score here: TOTAL:

The maximum possible score is 20. A score of 14 or above shows that you and your team have a very positive attitude towards customer care. A score of six or less shows a very poor attitude, which would certainly mean that your customers have a poor opinion of the service you provide.

Activity 35

■ Time guide 5 minutes

The questionnaire in the last Activity may have pointed to some particular problems in relation to caring for your customers. Make a note of them here, and outline briefly what action you can take to correct them:

Problems: _____

_____

_____

Action: _____

_____

_____

Attitude problems among your team members are basically a supervisory issue, and usually come down to the sort of example which you and other managers give, and the quality of the supervision which you provide.

**3.3
Behaviour**

Behaviour means what you actually do for (and to) the customer. Staff may have a very good attitude towards customers without knowing how to put this into practice.

Anyone who deals with customers must treat them the way they expect to be treated – which is promptly, efficiently and with respect. Customers do **not** like staff who are:

● scruffily dressed, badly groomed, or sloppy in their behaviour;

● inattentive, off-hand, rude, sarcastic or 'superior';

● lazy, slow, careless or uncommunicative.

45

Part C

Personal standards are important: it is difficult to show respect for the customer if you cannot demonstrate self-respect first! At the point of contact with the customer, this becomes very important. First impressions count!

Activity 36

■ Time guide 4 minutes

Your organization probably has a 'front person' of some kind (a receptionist, a secretary, or perhaps a security guard) who is the first point of contact with customers and other visitors arriving at your premises. Think about a new customer coming face to face with this front person for the first time. What would that customer expect him or her to do? List the first *three* things that should happen:

1. _____

2. _____

3. _____

The customer will expect a suitable greeting, and in particular:

1. to be given immediate attention;
2. to be given friendly signs (which should include a smile and eye contact)
3. to be greeted with friendly but polite words (such as, 'good morning, how can I help you?')

This is quite different from the reception I had from the book shop assistant in my earlier example. She made two basic errors:

● she failed to give me her attention;

● she failed to make eye contact.

In fact the signs she gave me were very unfriendly.

Activity 37

■ Time guide 6 minutes

Non-verbal communication, or 'body language' – the signals we send each other by the way we behave – is much more important than most people realize.

Imagine entering an unfamiliar office for the first time, and coming up to the reception desk. How would you interpret these examples of body language on the part of the receptionist?

1. The receptionist is on the telephone, and just waves vaguely at you and carries on the phone conversation.

2. The receptionist, who is busy typing at the back of the reception area, says 'Good morning, how can I help you?', but doesn't get up.

3. The receptionist greets you politely, but doesn't look you in the eye.

4. The receptionist greets you politely, without a flicker of a smile.

5. When you arrive, the man at the reception desk is lounging in his chair with his feet up, smoking a cigarette. However, he greets you in a polite and friendly manner.

46

None of these is satisfactory because in each case the receptionist is sending you *negative signals*.

■ The first one is telling you that the person on the phone is more important than you are.

■ The second is telling you that the typing he or she is doing is more important than you are.

■ The third, by not looking at you, is showing signs which to most of us suggest uneasiness, guilty feelings, or even dishonesty; when you look someone in the eye in a friendly manner, you are saying:

– I'm being open and straightforward with you;
– I'm paying you attention

■ The fourth, by not smiling, is showing signs of hostility; the smile is a very important human signal, which says

– 'Don't worry, I am friendly';
– 'I really *am* glad to see you.'

■ The fifth receptionist is revealing a sloppy attitude to his work, even if the greeting he delivers is in itself satisfactory.

You probably do not have responsibility for the reception area, but the lessons should be clear:

everyone who *meets* the customer must *greet* the customer;

what we *do* is as important as what we *say*.

We can sum up this section by offering four rules for meeting and greeting:

1. show the other person you have noticed them;
2. make eye contact;
3. smile;
4. greet them politely.

What could be simpler? And yet how many people seem incapable of performing this basic and natural human ritual!

4   Telephone contacts

A very high proportion of direct customer contacts come via telephone calls, when customers phone:

● to make an inquiry;

● to place an order;

● to make an appointment;

● to chase a job;

● to complain.

Some organizations, like British Rail, have entire departments whose only job is to provide customers with information, but there are many organizations where almost anyone can find themselves at the end of a phone call from an internal or external customer.

For that moment, for that customer, the person who answers the phone *is* the organization (or the department or section, if the caller is an internal customer). The reputation of the organization or department stands or falls on how well that one person copes with the customer contact situation.

Activity 38

■ Time guide 2 minutes

There are several big differences between customer contact on the phone and face-to-face contact, and when talking over the phone we need to bear these in mind. What would you say are the two most important differences?

1. _____

2. _____

1. Although the telephone is an important medium of communication, the problem with it is that *less communication takes place* than when you are talking face to face:

■ you can't see what the people you are talking to look like;

■ you can't see the expression on their faces;

■ you can't see what they are doing while they are talking to you;

■ you can't see what is going on around them;

■ you can't 'read' their body language to judge how they are reacting to you.

2. This means we have to compensate by *working a little bit harder* when speaking on the phone than we do in face-to-face situations.

Activity 39

■ Time guide 2 minutes

Suppose you have to phone another organization to ask about an order that has not materialized. The phone rings and someone picks it up. What do you think that person should say?

_____

_____

Because you can't see what is happening at the other end, you don't know for certain that you've got the right number, or who is answering. Also, telephone lines distort voices, and you can't always recognize the speaker even when you know them quite well.

I hope that you agree with me that the person who answers should start with a polite greeting ('good morning' or 'good afternoon' is quite enough), and then concentrate on providing sensible information:

■ stating the name of the organization or department that you have reached;

■ giving his or her name;

■ asking in a polite and friendly way how he or she can help you.

Is that the kind of quality of service your team members provide when they answer the phone? Or do they just say 'Hello' and let the other person guess who they've got through to?

**4.1
Taking the necessary
action**

The other big issues when answering the telephone are:

● whether you are able to deal with the call personally;

● and what you do if you can't.

Activity 40

■ Time guide 8 minutes

Try to suggest some simple rules for how your staff should behave in these circumstances.

1. The person who takes the call is able to answer the enquiry, though it isn't really his or her job to do so.

_____

_____

2. The person who takes the call is able to answer the enquiry but feels too busy to do so at that particular moment.

_____

_____

3. The person who takes the call is not able to answer the enquiry, but can transfer the caller to someone who is.

_____

_____

4. The person who takes the call is not able to answer the enquiry, and the person who is able to is not available.

_____

_____

Here are my suggestions, based on accepted 'good practice':

1. Can answer, but it isn't his or her job.

● *Unless there is a very strong reason for not answering, this person should take the responsibility for doing so and make the extra effort to satisfy the customer's needs.*

2. Can answer, but too busy.

● *The customer's needs should come first, so there would have to be a very strong reason for not answering there and then; if there is, this person should:*

   – apologize;

   – take the customer's name and number;

   – arrange to phone back within a stated time;

   – keep this promise.

3. Cannot answer, but can transfer to someone who can.

● *Customers generally hate being transferred; if someone has to do so, they should:*

   – tell the customer what they are doing;

   – explain to whom they are transferring them;

   – give that person the customer's name and details of the enquiry before making the transfer.

4. Cannot answer, and the person who can isn't there

● *This is the source of many grumbles from customers, because in this situation the customer is often asked to phone again without any guarantee of success, and messages taken often get lost; the person taking the call should:*

   – tell the customer the name of the person who can answer them;

   – promise to make sure that they will do so;

   – take down the customer's name, number and other details;

   – take responsibility for ensuring that the named person does return the call.

Simple enough, but we all have experience of people who:

● can't see why information is such an important part of customer service;

● won't take responsibility for doing that little extra bit of service that keeps a customer happy;

● don't keep the service promises that they make.

4.2 Competence

The final part of the ABC is competence – being able to give the answers and provide the service that customers require.

Customers will accept being efficiently transferred to a competent person, or being told that a competent person will phone them back. But it would be much better if the person who spoke to them in the first instance was able to provide a proper answer.

Of course, this isn't always possible, but supervisors should try to ensure:

● that phone calls are 'fielded' by people who can competently answer them;

● that members of the team are given the training and experience that will equip them to answer competently as soon as possible.

Failure to provide proper service on the phone is just one of many things that contribute to poor customer care, and which can easily result in a complaint.

5   Customer complaints

Every organization receives its share of complaints, and these days it could even be said that a complaints industry exists. Some organizations have their own complaints departments, while others, including the national gas, electricity, telephone and water utilities, are watched over by statutory authorities – such as Ofgas, Oftel, and Ofwat – whose job is to monitor complaints and urge action. These bodies may have the power to inflict financial penalties if complaint levels get out of hand.

Local government is likewise watched over by an 'Ombudsman', and MPs and local councillors play a similar role on behalf of their constituents.

Finally, of course, there is the Consumers' Association, which represent millions of private customers who are unhappy about the goods or services supplied by commercial organizations.

**5.1
Dealing with
complaints**

The most sensible approach to complaints is to prevent them, by providing the right products at the right time, in the right way and so on. But it is hard to eliminate them altogether.

Activity 41

■ Time guide 2 minutes

When a customer (internal or external) complains, what is your workteam's usual reaction? Tick the answer which best describes their usual behaviour and attitude.

1. They try if possible to ignore it, cover it up, or shuffle the problem off onto someone else. ☐

2. They become defensive, make excuses and even argue with the customer. ☐

3. They try to buy the customer off with compensation of some kind. ☐

4. They listen carefully and try to deal with the problem promptly and efficiently. ☐

5. They regard the complaint positively as an opportunity to strengthen links with the complaining customer. ☐

Here are my comments on these five positions:

1. They try if possible to ignore it, cover it up, or shuffle the problem off onto someone else.

   This is a very poor approach which does nothing to solve the customer's problem, and indeed may even make it worse, resulting in further complaints and more work.

2. They become defensive, make excuses and even argue with the customer.

   Although this reaction may seem 'natural', it is ineffective; the customer is not interested in excuses and arguing will only serve to irritate the customer further.

3. They try to buy the customer off with compensation of some kind.

   Staff who are embarrassed or frightened by a customer's complaint often try to offer compensation in the form of a rebate, a gift, or some extra service; this is not generally a good idea, because although the customer may accept it, it does nothing to put right the fundamental problem.

4. They listen carefully and try to deal with the problem promptly and efficiently.

   This is good – in fact a sympathetic hearing is the first thing a customer wants; it should be followed up with efficient handling of the problem.

Part C

5. They regard the complaint positively as an opportunity to strengthen links with the complaining customer.

This may sound odd: aren't complaints by their very nature negative?

Perhaps, but research has shown that they are also an opportunity. This is because, in British society, at least, most people do not like to complain directly. They are much more likely to say nothing and 'vote with their feet' by using another supplier next time.

Many large organizations now take the view that customers who complain are valuable assets who are worth cherishing:

- *they tell us about faults in our product or service of which we may not have been aware;*

- *properly treated, they become better and more loyal customers than those who do not complain.*

Customers seem to prefer a supplier who can recognise a problem and put it right efficiently to one who is always 'perfect'. After all, no one is perfect for ever, and you never know what will happen on the inevitable day when the perfection fails...

Complaints are also an important source of management information. In one large retail group staff send details of all complaints and goods returned by customers to a central computer. This is a daily routine. The information is analysed so that buyers can spot problems with particular products or particular suppliers and take prompt action to put them right.

**5.2
Anger and apologies**

Finally, those customers who not only have a complaint, but are angry about it.

This may seem the most difficult kind of problem to deal with, but really the answer is quite simple:

> deal with the problem first, and the anger will subside.

Corinne was quietly packing some parcels for despatch when Tom from sales burst in. He was absolutely furious. 'You stupid idiots,' he fumed, 'you knew perfectly well how hard we worked to get that order from Groby's, and you've gone and messed the whole thing up. They wanted ten complete sets of the Pascal software with all the manuals and interfaces, but you only sent them five sets, and you sent them to the wrong address. They should have been in Leicester yesterday, and you've sent them to Bath! Of all the drivelling incompetence I've ever met, this takes the biscuit! How on earth we are ever expected to sign up a new customer I really don't know. If you can't...'

'Oh dear,' said Corinne, 'no wonder you're upset. Let me just check the records and see what's happened...yes, look, we did send ten sets, but in two parcels. It looks as though Carters have only delivered one parcel. I'll get on to them right away to find out where the other one is.'

'But even if they find the other one, they're still in the wrong city! How in heaven's name did you manage to get that wrong?'

'I can't understand it, we always pull the despatch address straight out of the computer file,' said Corinne. 'Never mind that, though. The best thing is if I make up a new consignment and we'll despatch it by Securiteam on the priority overnight van. It'll be with them by ten in the morning.'

'Well, OK, I suppose that's the best we can do – but oh dear, what a shambles!'

52

'Yes, I'm really sorry, but I'll get on with it right away. Would you mind sending down the right address, and I'll make sure it goes in our records. I'll make a note to get Carters to return the original lot too.'

'OK then ... but **please** make sure this sort of thing doesn't happen again. I'll get on to Groby's and try and calm them down.'

A few minutes later, Tony phoned Corinne: 'Er, look, that address for Groby's, it looks like there may have been a mix-up at our end. There's no need to change the records. But can that new consignment still go out urgently please?'

'Yes of course,' said Corinne, smiling to herself. 'No problem!'

The basic rules for dealing with angry customers are these:

do
- listen;
- be sympathetic;
- concentrate on providing a solution to the problem;

don't
- offer excuses;
- argue;
- waste time trying to placate the customer's anger.

If you deal with the problem, the anger will soon go away. And remember, customers aren't always right, but you should treat them as if they were!

Self check 3

■ Time guide 15 minutes

1. Are these statements TRUE or FALSE?

   (a) Some employees never come into direct contact with a customer. TRUE/FALSE

   (b) When we are with a customer, what we do is as important as what we say. TRUE/FALSE

   (c) Contact on the phone is no different in principle from face to face contact. TRUE/FALSE

   (d) When a customer is angry or upset, you should concentrate first on calming them down. TRUE/FALSE

   (e) Customers who complain can be seen as a valuable asset. TRUE/FALSE

2. Unscramble the words in brackets so that these statement make sense:

   (a) (MAIN TIN ROOF) _____ is a very important part of customer service.

   (b) Always make sure that your service (RIPE MOSS) _____ are kept.

3. What is the ABC of personal service?

   A _____

   B _____

   C _____

continued overleaf

4. Complete these sentences by adding the missing half.

(a) When team members accept that customers are the most important people, then

_____

(b) When team members accept that satisfying customers' needs is the most important task, then

_____

(c) It is difficult to show respect for the customer if

_____

5. What messages are sent by these examples of body language?

(a) Avoiding eye contact.

_____

(b) Smiling.

_____

(c) Putting aside the work you are doing and approaching the customer.

_____

Response check 3

1. (a) Some employees never come into direct contact with a customer. This it TRUE, but it is unusual. Most employees occasionally have direct contact with a customer.

(b) When we are with a customer, what we do is as important as what we say. This is TRUE. Body language (non-verbal communication) is capable of sending powerful messages.

(c) Contact on the phone is no different in principle from face-to-face contact. This is FALSE. There are big differences, due to the fact that when we are on the phone we cannot see the other person.

(d) When a customer is angry or upset, you should concentrate first on calming them down. This is FALSE. The reverse is true: if you concentrate on dealing with the problem, this will automatically reduce the anger.

(e) Customers who complain can be seen as a valuable asset. This is TRUE. They tell us things about our product or service that we might not have realized, and properly treated they can become more loyal than customers who never complain.

2. (a) INFORMATION is a very important part of customer service.

(b) Always make sure that your service PROMISES are kept.

3. The ABC of personal service is:

> Attitude;
> Behaviour;
> Competence.

4. (a) When team members accept that customers are the most important people, then IT MAKES SENSE TO DO THAT LITTLE BIT EXTRA TO HELP THEM.

(b) When team members accept that satisfying customers' needs is the most important task, then IT MAKES SENSE TO GIVE SERVING CUSTOMERS PRIORITY OVER ALL THEIR OTHER TASKS.

(c) It is difficult to show respect for the customer if YOU CANNOT DEMONSTRATE SELF-RESPECT FIRST.

5. (a) Avoiding eye contact. This says you are feeling guilty, awkward or embarrassed, and that you don't want to give the other person your attention.

   (b) Smiling. This says you are friendly and are glad to see the other person.

   (c) Putting aside the work you are doing and approaching the customer. This says that you consider the customer is more important than the work you are doing.

6   Summary

- Most employees have at least some direct contact with customers, and should be trained in how to behave in a way that will please the customer.

- The quality of personal service depends on the ABC:

  Attitude;
  Behaviour;
  Competence.

- The basis of a good attitude is accepting that:

  – customers are the most important people in our working life;
  – satisfying their needs is our most important task

- The basis of good behaviour when in direct contact with the customer is to treat him or her with respect, in particular:

  – being smart and well-groomed (signs of self-respect);
  – giving them our immediate attention;
  – giving them friendly signs (including a smile and eye contact);
  – greeting them with friendly but polite words.

- Everyone who meets the customer must greet the customer.

- What we do is as important as what we say.

- When the contact is by telephone we need to make extra efforts:

  – stating clearly who and what we are;
  – taking accurate messages;
  – keeping customers clearly informed of what we are doing (for example when transferring them to someone else).

- Keeping promises is a vital part of customer care.

- When customers complain, deal with the problem, and any anger they feel will start to decline.

  do   – listen;
            – be sympathetic;
            – concentrate on providing a solution to the problem.

  don't   – offer excuses;
            – argue;
            – waste time trying to placate the customer's anger.

- Customers aren't always right, but we should treat them as if they were!

1   Introduction

It is impossible to deliver customer care successfully unless everyone in the organization is committed to doing so.

- If sales are committed, but despatch are not:
- If reception are committed but admin are not:
- If production are committed but stores are not:

then the result will be a failure to deliver.

Extension 1 Part D of the unit deals with how to achieve a commitment to delivering *total customer satisfaction* – a vital element in the drive to achieve the standards of quality that the modern world demands. For more details take a look at extension 1.

This will involve you in:

- checking how satisfied your customers currently are;
- identifying the problem areas;
- identifying the root causes;
- finding ways of overcoming them.

2   Identifying your customer care problems

Do you have a problem? Yes.

We can say this with confidence because:

- not even the most popular organizations get it right every time for every customer;
- customers' needs and expectations are always changing.

What is good enough today will not be good enough tomorrow. The most successful organizations believe in acting ***now*** to make sure they meet tomorrow's needs.

Absolute perfection is not possible. Our target for customer care should be continuous improvement towards perfection.

The first step is to identify the problem.

**2.1
Asking the customer**

Carisbrooke Cleaning Services provided contract office cleaning for numerous local firms. They were very competitive on price, and very responsive to their customers' complaints. Their policy was that whenever a customer complained, a supervisor and a back-up cleaner would arrive within two hours to check the problem and put it right. (Cleaning normally took place out of office hours.)

Many customers were impressed with the efficiency of this service, but as time went on, they became less impressed. Several customers began to ask CCS why their night cleaners couldn't do the job properly in the first place, and thus prevent the disruption involved in putting problems right during the day.

You may *think* you are providing an excellent service, but only your customers can tell you for certain. Many organizations now work quite hard to find out what their customers think of them. Here is part of a questionnaire issued by Cambridge Health Authority to try to find out how well they are meeting the needs of outpatients using the huge Addenbrooke's hospital.

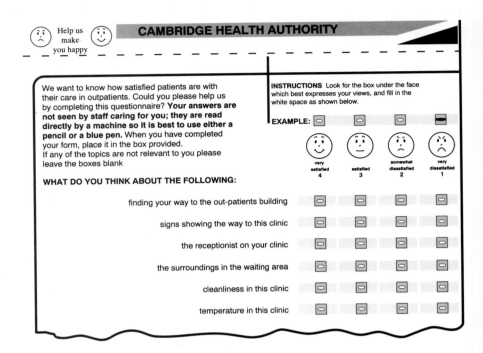

Reproduced courtesy of CASPE Consulting Ltd.

Health authorities deal with very large numbers of customers, so this form is designed to be 'scored' automatically using a computer, but this would not be necessary for smaller organizations.

Clearly, this is a serious exercise to find out what is right and what is wrong, so that action can be taken to improve the situation in the future.

Now let's put the spotlight on you, your department or section, and your team. It may not be your direct responsibility to satisfy external customers, so instead let's see how well you are satisfying the expectations of your internal customers.

Activity 42

■ Time guide 15 minutes

1. Choose one of your main internal customers from the list you made in Activity 14 on page 19.

2. Draw up a list of up to ten questions that you could ask, in order to find out how well you are satisfying this customer (we have suggested the first one for you, but change it if you wish). Try to put yourself in your customers' shoes, and ask the questions that will be most relevant to them.

The rating scale will help you measure how satisfied your customer is.

How satisfied are you with:	Very 5	Fairly 4	Moderately 3	Not very 2	Not at all 1

1. the speed with which we react to your requests?

2. _____

3. _____

4. _____

5. _____

6. _____

7. _____

8. _____

9. _____

10. _____

Of course, everyone who does this Activity will need to ask different questions, and the questions will probably need to be different for each different customer.

You will need:

■ to identify all the important aspects of the service you supply;

■ to be specific.

Asking a very general question such as 'How satisfied are you with our service?' will probably not tell you enough.

Here is an example of how one supervisor approached this Activity. The supervisor of the Word Processing Department of an insurance company decided to ask the questions below (the customer is a department which has direct contact with external customers).

Part D

How satisfied are you with:	Very 5	Fairly 4	Moder- ately 3	Not very 2	Not at all 1
1. the speed with which we turn round your documents?					
2. the system we use for logging your work in and out?					
3. the level of accuracy of our work?					
4. the way we deal with urgent jobs?					
5. the way we respond to queries from you on work scheduling etc.?					
6. our understanding of your technical requirements?					
7. our ability to meet special requests (such as extra copies, special paper etc)?					
8. the way we deal with you at the personal level?					

Are there any other points about our service that you would like to make? Please add them here:

_____

_____

_____

_____

Having read this, do you think that you ought to change any of your own questions before you try them out?

Activity 43

■ Time guide 30 minutes

1. Revise your short questionnaire if necessary, and write or type it up neatly on a clean sheet of paper. Discuss it with your line manager and get his or her approval to use it. (You may need to make further changes after this discussion.)

2. Now contact your customers, explain what you are doing and why, and give them copies of the questionnaire to complete.

**2.2
Looking at the results**

The ratings your customers give you may be good, bad or indifferent, but in most cases they will show that:

some aspects of your service are less satisfactory than others.

Your next task is to think carefully about the problem areas and consider how to deal with them.

Activity 44

■ Time guide 4 minutes

The WP department in our earlier example received the following ratings:

How satisfied are you with:	Very 5	Fairly 4	Moderately 3	Not very 2	Not at all 1
1. the speed with which we turn round your documents?		✓			
2. the system we use for logging your work in and out?		✓			
3. the level of accuracy of our work?	✓				
4. the way we deal with urgent jobs?			✓		
5. the way we respond to queries from you on work scheduling etc.?				✓	
6. our understanding of your technical requirements?			✓		
7. our ability to meet special requests (such as extra copies, special paper etc)?		✓			
8. the way we deal with you at the personal level?				✓	

Try to sum up what this questionnaire tells us, in a couple of sentences.

_____

_____

_____

As we saw in Part B, customer satisfaction factors fall into three groups:

● product-related factors (the right product at the right price);

● convenience factors (at the right place at the right time);

● human factors (in the right way).

Total customer satisfaction comes when all these factors are right.

The WP department's customers are quite satisfied with the product-related factors – speed, accuracy, ability to meet special requests. They are considerably less happy with the convenience and human factors – dealing with urgent requests (4), providing information (5), understanding the work (6) and personal contacts (8).

Problems have arisen when something is needed in a hurry – confirmation of details on an important policy, or authorization to carry out urgent spending, for example. In order to satisfy its external customers, the company needs to process such jobs more quickly than others, and here the WP department is letting the whole company down.

■ the staff aren't easy to talk to (this may include the supervisor);

■ they aren't flexible enough;

■ they don't provide enough information about work in progress.

Activity 45

■ Time guide 2 minutes

The WP department staff are seen as uncooperative, inflexible and uncommunicative. What would you suggest is the root cause of these shortcomings? Tick any of the following which you think may explain why these people behave the way they do.

The customers' demands are unreasonable.

The WP staff are naturally unfriendly and unhelpful.

The WP staff need more skill training.

The WP staff are unaware of what is required of them in terms of customer care.

Managers and supervisors are setting a poor example.

The company's policy in general is faulty.

1. The customers' demands are unreasonable.

   *Certainly not – the whole point of customer care is to satisfy the customer's demands as fully as possible. Customers are **not** always right, but they have to be treated as if they were!*

2. The WP staff are naturally unfriendly and unhelpful.

   Highly unlikely. Most people are naturally friendly and helpful – and there is no reason why this group of people should be any different.

3. The WP staff need more skill training.

   No – the problem is not one of skills, for which they received good customer satisfaction ratings.

4. The WP staff are unaware of what is required of them in terms of customer care.

   Quite probably. None of us performs properly when we don't know what standards are expected of us. The standards themselves may be quite simple, such as 'always answer the telephone within four rings', but they have to be set by management. This seems to be a problem in this particular case.

5. Managers and supervisors are setting a poor example.

   True. Here is what the department supervisor had to say on the subject:

   'We concentrate on doing the job we're told to do. We have high standards and we're pretty efficient. But we can't have people endlessly pestering us for information or trying to get something done quicker. That would just disrupt things and make our job more difficult.'

   If supervisors see customers as nuisances who make doing the job more difficult, then how can the staff be expected to treat them any differently?

   If supervisors don't see the need to make that extra effort, why should the staff?

6. The company's policy in general is faulty.

This may well be true. Many organizations still do not understand the importance of total customer satisfaction, or of the need to treat other departments as internal customers.

The problem with the WP department starts much higher in the organization:

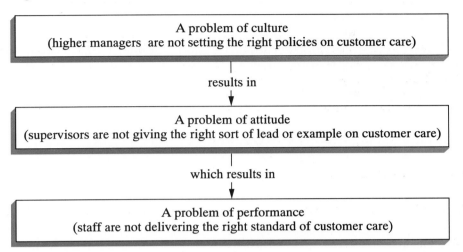

```
┌─────────────────────────────────────────────────────────────┐
│                      A problem of culture                      │
│ (higher managers  are not setting the right policies on customer care) │
└─────────────────────────────────────────────────────────────┘
                            results in
                               ↓
┌─────────────────────────────────────────────────────────────┐
│                     A problem of attitude                      │
│ (supervisors are not giving the right sort of lead or example on customer care) │
└─────────────────────────────────────────────────────────────┘
                          which results in
                               ↓
┌─────────────────────────────────────────────────────────────┐
│                   A problem of performance                     │
│  (staff are not delivering the right standard of customer care) │
└─────────────────────────────────────────────────────────────┘
```

2.4 Finding a suitable response

Here is a different situation, where the problem lies with product quality.

Redeye Ltd. makes outdoor lamps with PIR (Passive Infra-Red) detectors, which automatically switch the lights on for five minutes when someone approaches. Most of its products are sold through large retailers or by mail order.

A newly introduced model, the Redeye P3010, is causing problems. Roughly six percent of units sold are being returned to the retailers because the light fails to switch off again after the prescribed time.

Extension 2 The quality and safety of goods and services is covered by a number of Acts of Parliament. This Extension gives a brief summary of the law and a suggestion for further reading on this subject.

Like the earlier example of Carisbrooke Cleaners, The Redeye case study points to a quality assurance problem. Redeye's retail customers will be very unhappy with a product which:

● upsets their own consumers;

● loses them sales;

● involves them in extra administrative work.

Redeye *must* clear up this problem if it wants to succeed commercially.

Part D

Activity 46

■ Time guide 5 minutes

Redeye Ltd. has traced the quality problem to a rubber seal which is not properly seated, allowing moist air to get into the lamp's microcircuitry. This is an assembly problem, and the Production Manager has been told to sort it out. He calls the assembly line supervisors into his office.

The Production Manager knows that there are a number of different ways of tackling this problem of product quality. He makes the following list of options. Which do you think would produce the best results?

Option A. Tell the supervisors to 'get this problem sorted out pronto – I don't care how – or your necks are on the block.' ☐

Option B. Tighten up the quality control procedures so that faulty units are spotted before they are released. ☐

Option C. Set a new maximum target for failure rates of 0.25 per cent (one in four hundred units) and announce that in future no bonuses would be paid unless this target was met. ☐

Option D. Set a new target of 0.25 per cent, but offer extra bonuses when this target is met. ☐

Option E. Instruct the supervisors to find out which operatives assembled the faulty units and threaten them with disciplinary action. ☐

Option F. Ask the supervisors to discuss the problem with the more experienced members of the assembly team and report back with proposals for solving it. ☐

Option A would frighten the supervisors, who would then go down and frighten the assembly workers. This will not necessarily produce the desired result: it may even result in a reduction in quality, damaging morale and causing resentment.

Option B would reduce the number of faulty units leaving the factory, but it would increase costs without removing the fundamental problem.

Option C is in effect a financial punishment, and like all punishments is likely to produce resentment and resistance rather than better efforts and co-operation.

Option D is likely to have a better result, but it is a bad precedent to pay people extra for achieving a standard which after all is only satisfactory.

Option E also involves punishment, which could be seen as victimization, and is also likely to cause resentment. Everyone in the workforce is a volunteer, after all!

Option F is the best option: the benefits should be obvious. In the end, customer satisfaction is all about people. It is people who provide the services and people who make the goods. In order to ensure that they do so the right way, they need the right kind of supervision. That includes finding ways to give team members more responsibility for their work and widening their involvement in decision making.

3.1
A CASCADE of quality

In both production and services, one effective route to quality of service and total customer satisfaction is the CASCADE formula:

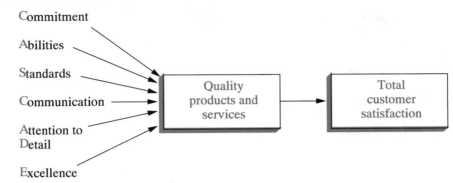

Commitment
Abilities
Standards
Communication
Attention to Detail
Excellence
→ Quality products and services → Total customer satisfaction

This really comes down to quality of supervision: it is the supervisor's task to achieve a CASCADE of quality towards customer satisfaction.

- *Commitment* to customer satisfaction from the workforce can only come if managers and supervisors demonstrate clearly their own commitment to it.

- *Ability* is crucial: staff must have the skills needed to perform to standard, whether they work in production, in a service capacity, or in direct customer contact roles.

- *Standards* must be set and measured, so that everyone knows what the target is and what more needs to be done to achieve it.

- Lack of proper *communication* between managers, supervisors and staff leads to misunderstandings, errors and dissatisfaction. No-one can produce a quality product in these conditions.

- *Attention to detail* marks the difference between those who only talk about customer satisfaction, and those who are really committed to succeed.

- *Excellence* is the result, if the formula is followed.

3.2
Commitment

Activity 47

■ Time guide 6 minutes

The Board of Directors of Hoplite Engineering Contracts Ltd decided that better customer care was the answer to an increasingly difficult competitive situation. They told the Managing Director to deal with the matter, and the MD told the Personnel Manager to devise a customer care training programme for the staff. The Personnel Manager drew up some rules for customer care, and issued them to all departmental managers, with the instruction, 'Bring these new rules to the attention of your staff.' Later, she brought in a lecturer from a local college to give groups of staff short talks on the subject.

The programme achieved very little. Why do you think this was?

_____

_____

_____

Any manager who thinks that customer care programmes are just a matter 'for the lower orders' is making a serious error. Customer care is a cultural issue, and it requires the whole organization to change its attitude. In order to work, a customer care programme:

■ must start at the top;

■ must involve everyone;

■ must have complete commitment from all levels of management.

Managers must demonstrate a clear personal commitment to customer care: if they don't set the right example, they can't expect the workforce to follow.

3.3
Ability (competence)

No-one starts life with the inbuilt ability to deliver customer satisfaction. We all have to learn the necessary skills, such as:

● the skill to machine a component to the right tolerances;

● the skill to clean an office to the right standard;

● the skill to prepare a report within the required time;

● the skill to handle a customer's complaint in the required manner.

Experience tells us that people who are fully competent in their work are more likely to be proud of what they do, and more likely to deliver a quality service.

This leads us to the conclusion that

quality customer care depends on ability and training.

Activity 48

■ Time guide 5 minutes

What steps might you take to improve your own and your team's ability to deliver a better quality of service? Try to suggest at least *two* steps.

_____

_____

You might consider:

■ getting yourself better trained, including perhaps learning to be a more effective trainer;

■ negotiating with your own manager or with your organization's training department to provide more training resources for your team;

■ looking for ways to expose team members more directly to customers, so that they can better understand their needs;

■ giving team members more responsibility for the quality of the products or services that they provide.

3.4
Standards and communication

In order to produce high-quality work that satisfies customers' expectations, people need to be told:

● what standards they are expected to achieve;

● how well they are meeting these standards;

● what effect their work is having on others.

Setting standards is relatively easy. Ensuring that they are understood and implemented calls for communication.

Communication is *not* just a matter of managers and supervisors handing down clear instructions. It also means listening to what the team members have to say, so that both sides can reach and share a common understanding of the situation.

It is a two-way process, and it should also be a continuous one, as the supervisor continuously monitors performance and provides feedback.

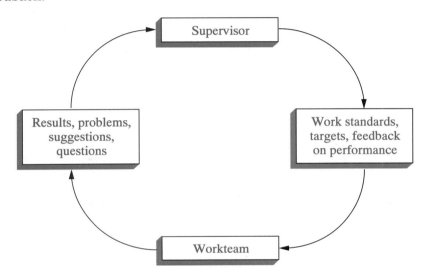

Activity 49

■ Time guide 2 minutes

Jot down the names of *three* kinds of people who need to communicate about the quality of the service provided to customers.

Customers, managers, supervisors and workteams all need to communicate about quality. You may also have mentioned others such as sales teams, customer support departments, quality control inspectors, and many other groups and individuals.

Whoever is involved, the communication needs to flow in both directions.

Activity 50

■ Time guide 3 minutes

Note down *two* or *three* kinds of information that you need to communicate to your own workteam about achieving a quality service and customer satisfaction in a particular job.

_____

_____

_____

As in many other aspects of work, supervisors may need to make sure that the members of their workteam understand:

■ what the job entails;

■ who the customer is, whether internal or external;

■ what the required standards or performance are;

■ how the job is to be done;

■ when the job is to be completed;

■ why it is needed.

In fact, when you think about it, all the information about a job has to do with quality, because to satisfy the customer, the job:

● must be done correctly;

● must be done on time;

● must be done thoroughly.

In other words, it must be done in a way which will satisfy all the customer's expectations.

Activity 51

■ Time guide 4 minutes

When you allocate work to your team members, how can you make sure that they have the same understanding of what the customer expects as you do? Describe the methods you think work best.

_____

_____

This will depend on how much understanding and trust already exists beween you and your workteam, and how experienced and competent the workteam's members already are.

With less experienced people it is often useful to ask them to explain back to you what they are required to do. Some supervisors make the mistake of assuming an understanding that isn't really there. It may not be enough at the end of a complicated instruction to ask, 'OK then – is that understood?' Even if you get a 'yes' or a nod of the head, it may not mean as much as you think!

3.5
Attention to detail

Total customer satisfaction doesn't appear by chance. It requires a great deal of thought and planning, and careful control of processes and functions.

Planning at the strategic level is usually the job of senior management. Detailed planning and control of individual tasks is usually delegated to supervisors, and this is where attention to detail is crucial. However high the commitment, and however good the intentions, it is attention to detail that:

- often makes one organization's products or services score over those of its competitors;

- makes the most lasting and loyal customers;

- puts the seal of quality on the work that you do.

4　Practical steps towards customer satisfaction

People are the most important resource of any organization, and in the final analysis, all questions of quality and customer satisfaction come down to how well these people perform. The big issue that faces every supervisor and manager in the world, is how to motivate people to work to the standards that are required.

4.1
Motivation

Motivation is not an easy subject, because everyone is different, and the things that motivate me will never be exactly the same as those which motivate the next person. However, both experience and research over many years have shown that some approaches to motivation work well, while others do not. Some approaches that seem sensible on the surface have a completely demotivating effect.

Activity 52

■ Time guide 4 minutes

How would you rate the following methods of motivating people to achieving high work standards?

I would rate this motiviation method as:

■ Paying them more money for better work.

Good	Poor	Fair

■ Leading by example – setting high standards for others to follow.

Good	Poor	Fair

■ Shouting at and threatening people when they perform badly.

Good	Poor	Fair

■ Showing recognition for effort and for excellence

Good	Poor	Fair

■ Setting targets that are meaningful and realistic

Good	Poor	Fair

■ Cultivating a team spirit by talking about problems and achievements in terms of 'us' and 'we', not 'you' and 'I'.

Good	Poor	Fair

continued overleaf

Part D

■ Showing that you care about and
believe in the task that the team
is trying to accomplish.

| Good | Poor | Fair |

■ Allowing people at all levels to attempt
to solve their own problems, rather than
have solutions imposed from above.

| Good | Poor | Fair |

See how your ratings compare with mine on each of these points.

■ Paying them more money for extra work.

Money is a motivator, but it has its limitations and drawbacks. People soon get used to increased income, and it ceases to motivate them. This can easily happen with incentive bonuses, which tend to end up being 'consolidated' in the wage packet. This can result in a worse problem – employees feel annoyed if the bonus is not paid for some reason. Money can easily become a dissatisfier rather than a motivator, so I would rate this approach no better than 'fair'.

■ Leading by example – setting high standards for others to follow.

I would rate this 'good'. You can't expect others to apply higher standards than you do yourself.

■ Shouting at and threatening people when they perform badly.

As we saw earlier, this is likely to have completely the opposite effect to what was intended, because it creates resentment. It is a poor way of motivating people.

■ Showing recognition for effort and excellence.

Praise works a lot better than blame, especially when it is done in front of others, so I would rate this as a good approach. Even a simple 'thank you' or 'well done' can work wonders.

■ Setting targets that are meaningful and realistic.

This also deserves a 'good' rating. Realistic targets give people something to aim at, and they make it clear what is required.

■ Cultivating a team spirit by talking about problems and achievements in terms of 'us' and 'we', not 'you' and 'I'.

You probably agree with me that supervisors ought to do this in all circumstances, as it is fundamental to creating a team in which people work together for a common goal. Another 'good' rating.

■ Showing that you care about and believe in the task that the team is trying to accomplish.

This too is an essential element of good leadership, and will also be effective in motivating people. I would rate it 'good'.

■ Allowing people at all levels to attempt to solve their own problems, rather than have solutions imposed from above.

Again, I would argue for a 'good' rating. It may take nerve for a supervisor to do this, but experience suggests that it can be a powerful motivator.

**4.2
Mobilizing the
workteam's skills
and knowledge**

Many managers think that their people are lazy and uninterested in their job, and that they have to be constantly chivvied in order to get a reasonable level of performance. But this is a vicious circle: people who are treated like this turn in a poor or lacklustre performance because they feel undervalued and underused, and because they never get a chance to speak or think for themselves.

A problem like the one in our Redeye case study raises this issue. Members of the workforce always know a good deal about the nature and cause of performance problems, but no-one asks their opinion, and this being the case, they see no reason to volunteer it. Often, they could offer a solution, but they simply aren't given the time or encouragement to think about the problems.

Why not let these people speak? Better still, why not let them work together to try to devise solutions to the problems that they have to deal with?

The case study shows the option which the assembly line supervisors at Redeye Ltd took.

Case
Study

Before the shift started the following morning, the supervisors took a group of the more experienced assembly workers aside and explained all about the faults in the P3010 and the dissatisfaction this had caused, and asked them if they had any suggestions. They explained that seating the rubber seal properly was rather tricky, and that newer workers always had difficulty with it. Also it was one of the last processes carried out, and if there was a lot of pressure to complete a batch, there was a temptation to skimp it.

Between them, the group decided:

1. to give new workers more time for training on this particular process;
2. that more experienced workers would keep an eye on their work;
3. that the supervisors would try to schedule workflows better, so that there were fewer situations in which work was likely to be skimped.

Organizations whose 'mission' is Total Quality often adopt this approach, by organising quality circles. This is what has started to happen at Redeye Ltd, although they haven't given their group a special name and it has so far only met once.

But if the solutions that the group came up with work, then this could become a regular Customer Satisfaction Circle!

As author Andrew Brown says of quality circles, the aim is not

'spontaneous, unplanned information group activity at shopfloor level. They should be a conscious and systematic attempt to tap the initiative, experience, creativity and collective wisdom of the rank and file employees, with full management support and participation.'

Extension 3 Andrew Brown's book *Customer Care Management* is mainly intended for more senior managers, but you will find much of interest in it. For example, he says that organizations which provide exactly the service that the customer expects should be rated not ten out of ten but zero! They should only score more when they provide more than the customer expects.

Activity 53

■ Time guide 10 minutes

Finally, let's return to your own Customer Satisfaction Questionnaire, and make a note of the areas of dissatisfaction. Think about how you and your team can deal with these issues and deliver a better standard of service.

Against each issue, make a note of what action you plan to take:

Area of dissatisfaction: Action to be taken:

_____   _____

_____   _____

_____   _____

_____   _____

_____   _____

It is always a good idea to get your team involved in talking about quality and customer care, and about their own problems in trying to deliver it. You may want to bear in mind, though, that a formal quality or customer satisfaction circle shouldn't be set up in isolation. To be fully effective, it needs the full commitment and backing of management; it may be advisable to discuss the idea with your own boss first.

Extension 4 If you would like to understand more about the way that quality circles work, there are several good books on the subject. A starting point might be to get hold of a copy of *In Pursuit of Quality*, by D. Hutchins.

5   A customer care culture?

To conclude Part D of the unit, think about the 'culture' of customer care that exists in your department or section and in the organization as a whole.

Activity 54

■ Time guide 2 minutes

To find out how far you feel your group (workteam, section or department), and the rest of the organization, are away from being able to provide total customer satisfaction, tick 'yes' or 'no' against the following questions.

	Within your group		Within the organization	
■ Is the word 'customer' used frequently?	Yes	No	Yes	No
■ Is there a clear commitment to customer care on the part of managers and supervisors?	Yes	No	Yes	No
■ Do people feel free to discuss the quality of customer service?	Yes	No	Yes	No
■ Are employees encouraged to bring forward their own ideas about improving quality of service?	Yes	No	Yes	No
■ Do managers and supervisors set high standards by personal example?	Yes	No	Yes	No
■ Are findings about customer satisfaction, levels of complaints etc. made available to employees?	Yes	No	Yes	No
■ Are clear standards or targets set for every aspect of quality and customer service?	Yes	No	Yes	No
■ When a problem arises, do the team members pool ideas to find a solution, rather than offering excuses or trying to blame one another?	Yes	No	Yes	No
■ Is the system for ensuring quality flexible and capable of dealing with new situations?	Yes	No	Yes	No
■ Is there generally a feeling of pride and achievement in the work that you do?	Yes	No	Yes	No

The more 'yes' answers you gave, the better you feel about the customer care culture in your workplace, and the more likelihood there is that total customer satisfaction is a serious issue in your working life.

If you feel that you and your team are setting higher standards in this respect than other colleagues, keep up the good work: your example can be an inspiration to others!

1. Are the following statements TRUE or FALSE?

(a) The only person who can reliably tell you what your customer care problems are is your line manager. TRUE/FALSE

(b) The customer is always right. TRUE/FALSE

(c) A customer care programme must start at the top. TRUE/FALSE

(d) Communication means making sure the workforce know what they have to do. It is basically a one-way process. TRUE/FALSE

(e) Customer care is all about personality. TRUE/FALSE

2. Unscramble the words in brackets so that these statements make sense:

(a) A customer care programme will not work unless it has total commitment from (TAN ME MEGAN) _____.

(b) Without proper standards, no-one can produce the right (FREE CORN MAP) _____.

(c) It helps if team members have more (PITY BORIS'S LINE) _____ for the quality of the products or services they provide.

3. What sort of problems do the following give rise to?

(a) Higher managers are not setting the right policies on customer care:

a problem of _____.

(b) Supervisors are not giving the right sort of lead or example on customer care:

a problem of _____.

(c) Staff are not delivering the right standard of customer care:

a problem of _____.

Response check 4

1. (a) The only person who can reliably tell you what your customer care problems are is your line manager. This is FALSE. Your line manager may well be right, but the only person who really knows for certain is the customer.

(b) The customer is always right. This is FALSE. There are times when customers are wrong, but you should always treat them as though they were right.

(c) A customer care programme must start at the top. This is TRUE. Without a commitment from every level of management, no customer care programme can succeed.

(d) Communication means making sure the workforce know what they have to do. It is basically a one-way process. This is FALSE. Communication is two-way: it is about listening to what the workforce have to say as well as telling them what they are required to do.

(e) Customer care is all about personality. This is FALSE. It is about ability, training, commitment, attitude and many other things, most of which the supervisor can influence.

2. (a) A customer care programme will not work unless it has total commitment from MANAGEMENT.

(b) Without proper standards, no-one can produce the right PERFORMANCE.

(c) It helps if team members have more RESPONSIBILITY for the quality of the products or services they provide.

3. (a) Higher managers are not setting the right policies on customer care:

a problem of CULTURE

(b) Supervisors are not giving the right sort of lead or example on customer care:

a problem of ATTITUDE

(c) Staff are not delivering the right standard of customer care:

a problem of PERFORMANCE

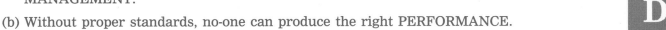

6   Summary

● No-one can afford to be complacent about the quality of customer care they provide:

– no organization is perfect;
– customers' needs are always changing.

● The only way to know for certain what your customers think of your service is to ask them.

● In both production and services, the CASCADE formula is an effective route to quality of service and total customer satisfaction:

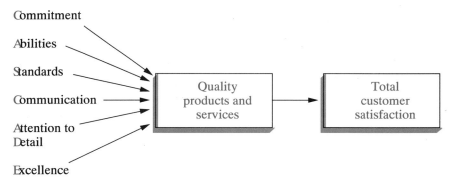

● Delivering customer care depends on the ability of higher management to establish a customer care culture:

– it must start at the top;
– it must involve everyone in the organization;
– it must have complete commitment from all levels of management.

● In order to produce high-quality work that satisfies customers' expectations, people need to be told:

– what standards they are expected to achieve;
– how well they are meeting these standards;
– what effect their work is having on others.

● Skilful supervision and a clear example is the key to providing total customer satisfaction at the level of the workteam.

75

1 Quick quiz

Well done – you have completed the unit. Now listen to the questions on Side one of the audio cassette. If you are not sure about some of the answers, check back in the workbook before making up your mind.

Write down your answers in the space below.

1 _____

_____

2 _____

_____

3 _____

_____

4 _____

_____

5 _____

_____

6 _____

_____

7 _____

_____

8 _____

_____

9 _____

_____

10 _____

_____

11 _____

_____

12 _____

_____

13 _____

_____

14 _____

_____

15 _____

_____

---

2   Action check

On Side two of the audio cassette you will hear four short scenes in which the issue of caring for the customer is raised. Listen carefully to the scenes and try to answer the questions raised at the end of each.

Write your answers and comments in the space below.

Situation 1:
Black pepper

_____

_____

_____

_____

_____

_____

Situation 2:
Excelsior's vans

_____

_____

_____

_____

_____

_____

Situation 3:
Who am I speaking to?

_____

_____

_____

_____

_____

_____

3   Unit assessment

Time guide 60 minutes

Case
Study

Read the following case incident and then deal with the questions which follow, writing your answers on a separate sheet of paper.

Darshana is a supervisor in the Payroll Section of a large retail group which has 16,000 staff scattered among more than 400 local branches. Monthly pay due is calculated manually by local branch managers, and the sheets are sent to Darshana's section for processing. Her staff code the sheets and enter the details into the computer, which issues the payslips and authorizes payments.

The section is always under heavy pressure, hours are long and staff turnover is high. Darshana is authorized to bring in 'temps' whenever the workrate justifies it, but a high proportion of the staff are always fairly inexperienced, and they have a high error rate. This results in a large volume of queries and complaints: the phone is constantly ringing as staff from all over the country try to find out why their pay is wrong. Darshana allocates her most experienced staff to dealing with these queries, which take an average of 14 minutes to sort out.

Often the phone lines are permanently engaged. Everyone is harassed and frustrated, the Payroll Section's reputation for 'customer care' is very low, and Darshana cannot see any way out of the situation. Her boss has suggested that one way of salvaging the section's reputation would be to give the staff who handle queries special training in customer care skills, and Darshana is considering this.

Darshana's position is a very difficult one. How would you approach it? Write *one* or *two* sentences in answer to these four questions.

1. What is the basic problem here?

2. Most of the payment errors only amount to a few pounds, and are almost all corrected within a month or two. Darshana cannot really see why her customers seem to get so upset about them. Can you suggest why this is?

3. What would you say to Darshana about her boss's suggestion of special training for the staff who deal with queries?

4. What action is needed to bring this problem under control?

Time guide 60 minutes

The time guide for this assignment gives you an approximate idea of how long it is likely to take you to write up your findings.

You will need to spend some additional time gathering information, perhaps talking to colleagues and thinking about the assignment. The results of your efforts should be presented on separate sheets of paper.

The purpose of this assignment is to make a thorough assessment of what you need to do in order to improve the quality of the care which your own department or section provides to its customers (both internal and external). You should think carefully about how you will lay out this information before beginning – it will need several columns.

1. List all the personnel in your team, including yourself.

2. Against each one, note down the role that they play in relation to their customers. If they have direct contact, describe this briefly (for example, whether face-to-face or on the phone; how frequently; in what capacity). If they have little direct contact, describe briefly how they contribute to serving the customer (for example, by providing services for others who do).

3. Rate each person on how well they perform their responsibilities in terms of delivering a quality service to the customer. Think about their:

● attitude towards customers and service;

● behaviour in practice;

● competence to deliver the right quality of performance.

Score them on a scale of 1 (low) to 5 (high).

4. Wherever you have made a low rating, indicate what action you will take to improve it.

And don't forget to include yourself!

1   Return to objectives

Now that you have completed your work on this unit, let us review each of our unit objectives.

You will be *better able to*:

● explain the meaning and significance of customer care;

    Customer care is a vital part of the marketing approach to success in the highly competitive modern world. Commercial organizations are under constant pressure to outdo their rivals, and even non-commercial organizations are under ever-closer scrutiny from government and various 'watchdog' bodies as well as from their own customers. A failure to meet customers' expectations threatens the survival of the organization and the jobs of its employees.

● identify your internal and external customers;

    Everyone is either serving external customers direct or serving those who are – internal customers. Many are doing both. Knowing who the customers are – and recognizing them as such – is the first step towards meeting their expectations.

● identify your customers' expectations and any areas in which you are failing to meet them;

    Immersed in doing our jobs, we often assume that we are doing what our customers want when we are not. We need to listen for customer dissatisfaction – monitoring complaints, for instance – but many dissatisfied customers do not complain. The only reliable way to find out how well we are serving our customers is to ask them, for example by using a questionnaire.

● provide an effective lead for your team in raising the standard of customer care which you provide;

    Almost every aspect of customer care, from the quality of the product to the way in which it is provided, comes down to people. These people do not deliver a quality service by accident: they need to be led, supervised and trained effectively within the right overall framework. The culture established by top management and the example provided by those at lower levels is therefore crucial.

● ensure that you and your team members perform to a high standard in customer contact situations.

    This involves: providing skilful supervision so that staff are well informed and well motivated and understand what standards are expected of them. It is the supervisor's job to ensure that their teams have the right attitude, behave the right way and have the skills needed to provide customers with the quality of service that they expect.

Extension 1

Details of BS5750: quality systems

BSI, the British Standards Institute, sets the target standards for the quality and specifications of many different products. If you work in an organization which produces (or trades in) manufactured goods, you will probably be familiar with the BSI 'kite-mark' and the standards for particular products.

BS 5750 (internationally known as ISO 9000) consists of a series of British standards that tell suppliers and manufacturers what is required of a system designed to deliver quality. They are intended to be practical standards which can be implemented by all sectors of industry.

The standards identify the basic disciplines and specify procedures and criteria ensure that products and services meet the customers' requirements.

Your organization may well already have details of BS 5750. If not, BSI publishes an introductory guide called *BS 5750/ISO 9000, 1987: A Positive Contribution to Better Business.*

Extension 2

Here is a brief summary of the role of the law in quality and the assurance of customers' rights.

The right of customers to goods and services of reasonable quality is enshrined in a number of Acts of Parliament, in particular:

● the Sale of Goods Act 1979;

● the Supply of Goods and Services Act 1982.

These apply to both business customers and individual consumers. They work by laying down general rules about the contract of sale which exists between a supplier and a customer. The key point is that customers are entitled to claim breach of contract and demand a refund if they are supplied with goods or services which are:

● not as described;

● faulty or of poor quality;

● unsuitable for their purpose;

● delivered unacceptably late;

● (in the case of services) carried out without due skill and care.

Customers can also sue for damages if they suffer additional losses as a result of the breach of contract (for example, if a poor quality delivery has to be rejected and the customer loses business thereby).

The law says that in these circumstances the customer can claim a refund because the supplier has invalidated the contract of sale. There are also circumstances where the product or service is below standard in some limited way but not so poor as to invalidate the contract as a whole. Here the customer can demand a reduction of the price as a condition of allowing the contract to stand.

The private consumer who buys faulty goods or services has a 'strict' right to a refund from the retailer who sold them. It is 'strict' in the sense that the retailer is obliged to pay up even if the fault lay entirely with the manufacturer and was something which the retailer could not possibly have known about. (Of course retailers in turn can claim against their own suppliers.)

In retailing, quality of customer care is of vital importance, and retailers try to do everything possible to ensure that their customers' legal rights are met promptly, politely, and without raising objections.

The Consumer Protection Act 1987 gives more rights to the private consumer. It deals with products that have hidden faults that cause damage or loss to the customer (such as a faulty fountain pen that leaks and ruins a suit). The Act introduces the concept of 'product liability' to English law. This allows the customer to obtain damages for loss or damage direct from the manufacturer or importer (if the item was made outside the EC). The retailer only becomes liable if unable to identify the manufacturer or importer (though retailers are responsible for their 'own brands' as if they were manufacturers).

Before this Act was passed, customers' position was weaker: they had to rely on the old principle of negligence (or the 'duty of care'). This stated that the customer could only claim damages if he or she could prove that someone had been negligent – which was usually very hard to do. Now that product liability has arrived, customers no longer have to prove that anyone was negligent, but only who made, imported or supplied the goods.

The Consumer Protection Act 1987 also deals with product safety, and there are numerous other laws and regulations on this subject. If your organization supplies goods and services commercially you should make sure that you have a thorough understanding of the regulations concerned.

The Citizens' Advice Bureau publishes a series of free booklets and pamphlets which explain consumers' rights in straightforward language. You will find a local address in your telephone directory.

Extension 3

Book:	*Customer Care Management*
Author:	Andrew Brown
Publisher:	Butterworth/Heinemann, Oxford, 1989

Extension 4

Book:	*In Pursuit of Quality*
Author:	D. Hutchins
Publisher:	Pitman, London, 1990.

These Extensions and the videos can be taken up via your Support Centre. They will arrange for you to have access to them. However, it may be more convenient to check out the materials with your personnel or training people at work – they could well give you access. There are other good reasons for approaching your own people as, by doing so, they will become aware of your continuing interest in the subject, and you will be able to involve them in your development.

ACTION PLAN

Work out your own plan of action for improving the quality of the customer care which you and your team provide by responding to the following check questions and picking up the ■ action prompts.

Check questions   Your response and intended action

1. Can you explain to your team why customers are of such importance to your organization?

_____

_____

_____

■ *You must be able to convince your team members of the degree to which the success of the organization and their personal futures are dependent on the customer. Why not write down the key points you would make to them?*

2. If you work in a non-commercial organization, do your team members clearly understand why the people you serve should be regarded as customers?

_____

_____

_____

■ *You can find out in discussion, or perhaps with an 'attitude questionnaire' like the one we used in Activity 34. If you are not confident about their attitude, you should draw up a plan for changing it, using personal example, individual briefings, and perhaps group training sessions.*

3. Do you and your team have a clear understanding of what business you are in?

_____

_____

_____

■ *You are in the business of meeting your customers' needs. It is your job to decide what these are, and to make sure your team recognize them too.*

4. Have you identified your internal customers, and do you make an effort to serve them as well as an external customer might expect?

_____

_____

_____

■ *You will also be the customers of other internal departments. Think about the service they provide, and how they could do better. Consider the service that you supply to your own internal customers in the light of this.*

5. Do you have a clear picture of the various factors which contribute to 'customer satisfaction' among your own customers?

_____

_____

_____

■ *It is important to work out what these factors are and to brief your team on them. You should be feeding back information of this kind to your team constantly.*

85

Action

6. How well does your team understand the customer's needs and expectations?

_____
_____
_____

■ *It is always useful to understand more about your customers. Discuss with your boss ways of opening up more direct contacts between team members and customers.*

7. What steps have you taken to ascertain how well you are satisfying your customers' expectations?

_____
_____
_____

■ *As we showed in Part B, the only way to know for sure is to ask the customers. You can do this by talking directly with them, but it is a good idea to draft out beforehand the most important questions you should ask.*

8. What are you doing to provide customers with that little bit of extra service which makes all the difference?

_____
_____
_____

■ *Every customer's needs will be different, but the 'little extra' might be something as simple as phoning regularly to check that what you have done for them is satisfactory.*

9. How well do you and your team handle face-to-face customer contacts?

_____
_____
_____

■ *You should observe your team members in contact situations and decide what improvements are needed. You may need to discuss ways of improving standards with your own manager, or your organization's training department.*

10. How well do you and your team handle contacts with customers over the telephone?

_____
_____
_____

■ *You should listen to your team members talking on the telephone in contact situations and decide what improvements are needed. You may need to discuss how to deal with these with your own manager, or your organization's training department.*

11. How well do you and your team handle complaints from customers?

_____
_____
_____

■ *Again, you should observe carefully how team members behave when they receive complaints. You may need to arrange one or more training sessions as well as talking to people individually.*

12. **Have you devised a questionnaire and used it to establish how satisfied your customers are, and what their specific areas of dissatisfaction are?**

■ *We gave you guidelines for assessing customer satisfaction in Part D. You may prefer to test your questionnaire on one of your friendliest customers before using it more widely.*

13. **Have you taken steps to improve the level of satisfaction among your customers?**

■ *In order to improve the level, you will need to think carefully about which factors are most important, and to concentrate on improving these.*

14. **Are your staff competent to deliver the right standard of customer service?**

■ *Quality customer service depends on the people concerned performing their jobs to the right standard. You should consider making a broad-based review of your team's skills and performance and arranging extra training where there are shortfalls.*

15. **How can your team make a positive contribution to strengthening the customer service 'culture' in your organization?**

■ *Caring for customers and providing the right standard of quality service requires a team approach. Your team can make a significant contribution to the all-round raising of standards by setting an example to others.*